1&2 COLOR DESIGN COLLECTION 1

Effective design using only 1 & 2 colors

PIE
BOOKS

1 & 2 Color Design Collection 1

PIE BOOKS

2-32-4, Minami-Otsuka, Toshima-ku, Tokyo 170-0005 Japan
Tel: +81-3-5395-4811 Fax: +81-3-5395-4812
e-mail:editor@piebooks.com
        sales@piebooks.com
http://www.piebooks.com

ISBN4-89444-454-2 C3070
Printed in Japan

本書は好評につき完売した「1＆2色グラフィックス」の改訂版です。
序文は上記タイトルのために書かれたものをそのまま使用しています。

This book was previously published in a popular hardcover edition entitled "1 & 2 Color Graphics".
References to the title in the foreword of hence reflect the original title.

contents

イントロダクション

『1色&2色デザイン』ということについて、6人のデザイナーの方に自由にコメントしていただきました。共通していたのは、色数の限定という一見ネガティブな条件を制約とは考えず、様々な可能性を追求する場としてポジティブにとらえている点でした。

『2色>4色』 Cyan

サイアンの活動は文化的な分野に限られています。予算が限られているからということもありますが、これらのプロジェクトにおいては、手の込んだ複製技術やリトグラフ、4色印刷は過去のものとなりつつあります。そこで私たちは1色&2色印刷のあらゆる可能性を追求し、色々な実験を試みます。またこの限られた方法で制作することは、私たちにとっては美的探究という意味でもやりがいがあります。加えてこれは環境保護の側面からも重要であり、フィルム、印刷版、化学薬品などを節約したり、適切な印刷用紙を選ぶことは大切なことです。私たちの考えでは、『リアルさ』を『完璧』に再現し、紙の上にコピーして人々を過剰に刺激するという方法は、もはや無効になっています。ハイテクイメージの外交員が登場するあらゆる保険会社のケバケバしたパンフレットや、『我が家こそ我が城』的な住宅金融組合の雑誌に描かれたイラストは、美的・技術的に可能な方法を使い尽くしてしまいました。私たちはこのような観点から出発し、内容・官能性・本質的美を統合する方法と、また、時間が経った後も鮮やかに記憶に残るようなデザインの手法を捜し求めています。さらに過剰な科学薬品を使用しなくてすむ素材も探しています。天然紙では色の写りや印象が違ってくるので、デザイン表現の組み立てを変える必要があります。クライアントとのブリーフィングの中でこうした諸々の問題について議論するのですが、なかなか理解してもらえないこともあります。予算が限られているにも関わらず、クライアントはカラフルで光沢のあるものを求めることが多いのです。私たちはこれまでに、天然紙の上で2色を混ぜ合わせたり塗り重ねたりすることを随分くり返してきましたが、これは今なお実に興味深い実験であり、最終的な色は印刷機にかけた時に決まるのです。

オフィスプロフィール:サイアン
「サイアンの創作物はそのコンセプトにおいて、1920年代から30年代初期にかけてのアヴァンギャルドデザインを志向するものであり、また見る者に知覚・経験する能力を開発する機会を提供する視覚的文化を提案するものである。(中略)サイアンは写真を巧みに合成し組み合わせる手法を自在に駆使し、多用します。しかしながら同様に、最新の表現環境の中で古き良きボドニを取り入れたり、文化的伝統から美的緊張を生み出したり、テクストとイメージと紙を融合させてファーストフード広告戦略に対抗しうる独自の存在物を創り出す能力も持ち合わせます。」J.ベトルシャット博士―ノヴム誌(ドイツ・デザイン誌)/94年2月

『メッセージを色で伝えるということ』 Stoere Binken Design

私たちは1色または2色の制作を楽しんでいることが殆どです。なぜならフルカラー印刷では失われがちな美的純粋性や抽象性を持たせることができるからです。もちろん1&2色の作品にはクライアントの資金を大幅に節約するという、もう1つの(同じように重要な)側面もあります。このことが限られた刷り色で制作する主な理由であることも少なくありません。

2色で制作する場合、色の彩度を思いどおりにコントロールすることができます。2色のかけ合わせによりたくさんの色のグラデーションを作ることができます。このようにして平面でありながら緻密に層をなす作品を作り出し、作品に独特の雰囲気を生み出し、見るものの感情に訴えかけます。

こうやって色の試行錯誤を続けると'良いデザイン'の核心に触れられそうになります。―それは、伝えようとするメッセージが非常にストレートで、しかも嘘がなく、かつ奥行きがあるということです。優れたデザインとは美しいだけのものを作ることではなく、クライアントの意図にかなうグラフィック言語を生み出すことなのです。

残念なことですが、最近の著しいマルチメディアブームにおいては、デザインはごまかし的で現れてはすぐ消えるフルカラーイメージとなり、もはや人目を引く以外の能力が無くなりつつあるように思います。この過程でメッセージが押し潰されてしまうことが非常に多いのです。

オフィスプロフィール:ストーレ・ビンケン・デザイン
オランダのマーストリヒトにある比較的若いグラフィックデザインスタジオ。親友である2人から成る。アカデミー・オブ・ファインアーツ・マーストリヒトを卒業後さまざまに活動を始める。国内外においてさまざまなクライアントを持ち、内容はCI、CDジャケット、雑誌、フライヤーなど多岐に渡る。「私たちはデザインに対して独自のビジョンを持っています。だからクライアントは私たちを選んでくれるのです。」

『見慣れたものを見慣れないものへ』 Sean O'Mara

自分の個性を商業デザインの中でいかに表現するかという私の考え方は、記号論を学んだ時に根底から覆されました。何よりもまず、組み合わせが意味と解釈を定義するということに気づいたのです。日常的にデザイナーが使用するグラフィック言語(対象/紙/イメージ)をまったく新しい視覚的組み合わせの中で使うことが、見慣れたものを見慣れないものへ変える方法であり、また自分の中にある強烈なイメージをデザインの中で表現する1つの方法になりました。

本書に掲載されている私の作品は、視覚的な組み合わせを弄び、日常見慣れているはずの要素で、まったく新しい別の意味を伝えようとしています。つまり、通り一遍の意味の中で生活している人々の中に驚きや違和感が生じれば、私の意図したことは100%達成できたと言えます。

商品を魅力的に見せようとする言葉(つまり広告)は、受け手を引きつけ、"思考"を喚起するものであって欲しいものです。グラフィックデザインとは、言葉と絵によってアイデアを視覚的に結びつけ、消費者のニーズを明確に表現しようとするものです。多くの場合商業デザイナーは、テーマを与えられるとそれに沿った要素を集め、テーマに最も合うように、時に冒険的に組み合わせます。しかしながら、一方的にアイデアを伝えてモノを売ろうとすることに終始し、相手から何かを引き出そうとすることはありません。デザインすることの最終的な目的は、見る者に思考を喚起させ、メッセージを理解させることであり、かつ作品に個性を持たせることにあります。受動的にではなく、主体的に見させることがグラフィックデザイナーの仕事なのです。

プロフィール:ショーン・オマラ
1967年オランダ生まれ。1985―90年 ダンレアラ・カレッジ・オブ・アート・アンド・デザイン(ダブリン)卒業。1990年 Xon Corpデザインスタジオ(ダブリン)設立。1991―93年 セントラル・セントマーティンズ・カレッジ・オブ・アート・アンド・デザイン(ロンドン)卒業/修士号取得。1993―95年 イマジネーション社(ロンドン)/シニアデザイナー。現在、ボディ・ショップ・インターナショナル(ロンドン)でシニアデザイナー兼マネージャーを務める。

『2色であることの理由』 Darin Beaman

私たちの仕事の60%以上は、1色ないし2色しか使用していません。これはアートセンターが非営利の学術団体で、予算が限られているためです。予算が限られるとデザインも制約を受けると考える人もいますが、私たちはいかなる印刷物も私たちの視覚言語を開発し、発展させる良い機会であると考えています。

例えば本書に掲載されている『Objects』展カタログです(P132)。この展覧会は出展作品数も予算も多くはありませんでしたが、テーマはとても高尚で、私たちに完全にオリジナルな解答を求める命題のようでした。このカタログの形態はオブジェとしての本を表現しています。綴糸とチーズクロスを露出させて、製本過程の一部としての物質性を強調しました。ハードカバーをはずし、各本文ページには表紙と同じ紙を用いて、本の「非具体化」ということに徹底しました。こうして、本と単なるモノとの境界線を微妙に混乱させたわけです。

このような小規模のプロジェクトでは、既成の概念に捕らわれない自由な発想が必要とされます。私たちはこのようなプロジェクトにとてもこだわります。なぜなら、こうした手法が私たちを未知の方向へ、また新しい方法論へと導いてくれるかもしれないからです。

オフィスプロフィール:
1986年、アートセンター・カレッジ・オブ・デザイン学長デーヴィッド R.ブラウン氏がデザインオフィスを設立。カレッジのすべての印刷物を担当。1987年以降、副学長兼クリエイティブディレクター、スチュアート・フロリック氏がデザインオフィスを管理している。1991年、カレッジ専属デザイナー、ダリン・ビーマン氏が加わる。本書の掲載作品は、2人のアートディレクターと5人のデザイナー、プロジェクトのための制作スタッフにより5年がかりで制作されたもの。

『色の記憶』 Jean-Benoît Lévy

今これを読んでいるあなたは、何色が好きですか？私の好きな色はその時の気分や、たぶん季節によっても変わります。

昼、夜、そして移ろいやすい光の中で、色は常に自己主張し、その周囲にあるものと対立しています。デザインにおいては、写真やタイポグラフィの選択と同様に色の選択は最も重要です。色はその色が発する雰囲気と共に存在します。これが分かれば問題はもはや「なん色使うか？」ではなく「どの色を使うか？」になります。

バーゼルの劇場ポスターシリーズを制作した時は、私はまず初めに実際の作品を読み、デザインと劇の内容が調和するようにしました。私は作家が作品の初めに特定の場所（街・森）・時間（朝、夜...）・背景（家の中、屋外）を示し、１つまたは複数の色を仄めかす場合が多いことに気づきました。

また、私は常に、自分の周囲にあるもの、自分の目に映るものの影響を素直に受け入れるようにしています。－ファッション、他の人のグラフィックデザイン、斬新なフライヤー、そして自然の中の、あるいは画筆を洗っている時に偶然に生まれる面白い色のコンビネーションなどです。私はこのような「視覚の決定的瞬間」を重要だと感じ、この「色の記憶」を意識し、忘れないように努めます。

アートディレクションが定まった後も色はなお発展し続け、製作時まで続くことさえあります。最終的に色調・明度・濃度・彩度が決まるのはプレスチェックの時です。そして完成したポスターが街に貼られているのを見た時に、やっとその色の選択が正しかったかどうかが分かるのです。

今日あなたはどんな色の組み合わせを身につけますか？よく選んでください。色はあなたの個性を反映することもあるのですから！

プロフィール：ジャン＝ベノワ・レヴィ
１９５９年生まれ。１９７８－８３ デザイン・カレッジ（バーゼル）卒業。１９８３－８６ スイス・フェア（見本市）にてデザイン担当。１９８７ ローザンヌにて定期誌２誌のエディトリアル・デザイン担当。同年６か月間フリーランス。１９８８ And, Trafic Grafic 設立。１９９１年以降、アートセンター・カレッジ・オブ・デザイン・ヨーロッパ、デザイン・カレッジ（バーゼル）、アメリカのRISDにて講師を担当。現在はデザイン／広告の分野にとらわれず活躍。最近ではスイスPTTの切手をデザインする。

『デザインのウラのデザイン』
Makoto Orisaki

おもに色数の制約は予算によるものだろうが、私はそれらがクリエイティブの制約にならないことの実践として、絵柄のデザインを越え、分野外素材やミシン目などの特殊加工を施している。この場合には仕入から物流、技術、そして理解ある工場（職人）のセッティングとコスト設計がすべてである。本来のグラフィックデザインの外にあるもののようだが、この作業無くしては実現しない。その結果として予算内での新たな試みや、異業種間の交流がなされている。

日本人の紙に対する質感、価値観を問う意味も含め、数年前から産業用紙（板紙、ボール紙etc.）を使ったデザインを試みている。マルチメディアでは今のところ表現できないリアルな情報である触感、質感は紙媒体の重要点ととらえている。日本の印刷用紙は印刷適正にとらわれすぎた画一的な紙が多く、もっと表情豊かな紙（再生紙）があって欲しいと考える。自ら開発生産にかかわれたらと考え、実体験のマーケティングとして、ＤＭ作りを最も有効な実験の場としている。最近では製造・再生・美的にも有利であると考え、究極の０色デザインを仕掛けている。

プロフィール：織咲 誠
１９６５年生まれ「デザインで"自己表現する"ということには全く興味ない。ただいつも気に留めているのは『ヒューマンエラー』というコト。何かを形にし、社会に出すという行為はあらゆるもの（価値観、文化、生活etc.）に対してなにがしかの影響を与えることになりうるので、責任ある立場をとりたい。デザインするということは、洞察眼を持ち、すべて（機能、心身、環境、美、ユーモアetc.）に対してベストな状態を導き出す行為と考えている。そのようにして生み出されたものは、必然として個を越える。」

INTRODUCTION

As an introduction to this collection, we offer here the comments of six designers on the subject 'design with one or two colors'. They share the view that a limitation on the use of color should be seen not as a handicap, but as an opportunity offering a wealth of potential to explore.

"two > four" cyan

cyan works exclusively in the cultural sector. for these low and no budget projects, the question of elaborate reproduction techniques, lithography and 4c printing is mostly obsolete. thus we try to use all possibilities of one and two colour printing and to experiment with these. moreover it is aesthetically interesting for us to work with these minimal means. in addition, the ecological aspect is important. we consider it important to save film material, printing plates, chemicals etc. and to use adequate printing paper... the over stimulation with <<perfectly>> reproduced and printed <<reality>> is in our opinion used up. high-tech quality of images for the employees of any insurance broker in a glossy ad brochure or the illustrations for a <<my-home-is-my-castle>> building society magazine have overstrained the technical and aesthetical possibilities. starting from this point we look for solutions which are a unity with regard to content, sensuality and aesthetics and which do not wear off or disappear after one single brief glance. moreover we look for materials which exclude the use of superfluous chemicals. natural papers ask for a different style of work on images as colours print and look differently. during briefing, all this is discussed with the clients who are sometimes not easily convinced. often they want, in spite of limited finances, something colourful and glossy. even though we have plenty of experience in mixing and layering two colours on natural paper, it still remains a most interesting experiment, and the final colours are fixed at the printing machine.

Office profile: cyan
"cyan describes its conceptual planning as traditionally slanted toward the design avant-garde of the twenties and early thirties, as proposal for a visual culture in which the individual's ability to perceive and experience is given a chance to develop. [...] this explains its preference for photography, its masterful manipulation of montage and dissolve techniques. but there's also the ability to include good old bodoni in a completely new expressive environment, to transform cultural traditions into aesthetic tensions, to weld text, image and paper into a single entity that can stand up against fast food ad ploys." by dr. j. petruschat in novum (german design magazine) 2/94

"Communicating the client's message through colour"
Stoere Binken Design

More than often we prefer to work with one or two colours because it gives an aesthetic purity and abstraction to the artwork that you often lose with full colour printing. Of course, another (no less important) aspect of one & two colour work is that it saves the client lots of money. Many times this is the main reason for working with limited colours.

Working with two-colour artwork gives you total control over the intensity of the colour. The fusion of two colours produces other colours that can be varied into numerous gradients. In this way you can create densely layered artwork that is less 2-dimensional, that creates an atmosphere and stimulates the emotions of the viewer.

Experimenting with colour in this way brings us closer to what good design is all about; communicating the message in a very direct, honest and profound way. Good design is not about making beautiful things, but creating a graphic language that serves the intentions of the client.

Unfortunately, the recent multimedia explosion has set the decor for designs with flashing, rapidly changing full colour images that are merely used to get the viewer's attention. Too often the message is suffocated in this process.

Office profile: Stoere Binken Design
We are a relatively young graphic design studio, stationed in Maastricht, the Netherlands. Our studio consists of two good friends. We started off directly after graduating from the Academy of Fine Arts Maastricht. We operate on an (inter)national level and have a variety of clients. Our work varies from corporate identities, CD sleeves, to magazines, flyers, etc. We have our own vision about design and that's why clients choose us.

"The Object of Two Colors"   Darin Beaman

More than 60 percent of the projects at Art Center are one- or two- color. This is due to the limited budgets in a nonprofit academic environment. Some think that these limitations also limit the design, but we see any printed piece as an opportunity to develop and expand our visual language.

An example of this is the *Objects* exhibition catalog (pg.132), which is featured in this volume. The quantity and budget were small, but the subject matter was rich; it seemed to demand a unique solution. The form of the catalog addresses the notion of the book as object. We exposed the binding threads and cheesecloth to emphasize their materiality as part of the book production process. We stripped the catalog of its hard cover and used cover stock for the text pages, continuing the strategy of "dematerializing" the book. These elements were combined to create a subtle category confusion between book and object.

We are compelled to take risks and explore unconventional conceptual and production options on smaller projects. We remain committed to their every detail because we never know where they will take us—or what new thinking they may inspire.

Office profile: Design Office for Art Center College of Design
Founded in 1986 by President David R. Brown, Art Center's Design Office is responsible for all the college's printed material. Stuart Frolick, vice president and creative director, has supervised the office since 1987. Designer for the College Darin Beaman joined Art Center in 1991. The work represented in this volume was completed over a five-year period by two art directors, five designers, and a limited production staff.

"Remembrances of Colors"
Jean-Benoît Lévy

What's your favorite color, you who are reading this text? Personally, mine changes according to my mood or maybe the season.

By night, day and in any type of light a color is constantly in confrontation with its surroundings. Just as photography and typography, the selection of color is essential. Colors exist by the feelings they exude. Once this is determined, the question is no longer, "how many colors?", but "which colors?".

In the case of the theater poster series I created for Basel, I first read the actual works before starting so that my design would correspond to the performed pieces. I found that authors often begin their texts by indicating specific location (a town, a forest), a time of day (morning, evening...), a setting (in a house, outdoors) and allude to one or more colors.

I also allow myself to be influenced by what I see around me: fashion, other graphic designs, innovative flyers, interesting combinations in nature and even accidentally when washing out my paint brushes. Aware of the importance of these "visual moments", I try to hold on to "remembrances of colors".

After an artistic direction is taken, the colors still continue to evolve, even up until production. It is with the printer on the presscheck that the last decisions of tone, transparency, deepness and saturation are made. And later, when I see the poster hung out in the street, I can finally see if the color choices were the right ones.

What colors will you wear today? Choose them well because they may also be the reflection of your personality!

Profile: Jean-Benoît Lévy
Born 1959. Schule für Gestaltung (College for Graphic Design), Basel 1978-1983. Graphic designer at Schweizer Mustermesse (Swiss Trade Fair) 1983-1986. Magazine designer for two periodicals in Lausanne, summer 1987. Freelancer in San Francisco for six months, 1987. Foundation of own studio "And, Trafic Grafic", summer 1988. Lecturing at Art Center College of Design Europe 1991-1996 and at Schule für Gestaltung, Basel 1993-1994. Guest lecturer at Rhode Island School of Design, Providence, USA, winter 1995-1996. Current work encompasses the complete spectrum of graphic design and advertising. Has just produced a postage stamp for the Swiss PTT.

"Making Strange"   Sean O'Mara

My ideas about how to introduce personality into the commercial design model were turned upside down when studying semiotics, the theory of signs. I found context, more than anything else, defines meaning and interpretation. Using the graphic language of every day forms (found objects/papers/images) in entirely new visual contexts, became a way of making strange familiar messages, and introducing personal obsessions into design work.

Included in this book are some of my designs that play with context, and attempt to use familiar language to carry unfamiliar meanings. Ultimately, I want to provoke a reaction from the viewer who may not anticipate ambiguity.

The discourse of commercial seduction is used, hopefully, to inspire the viewer to look closer and THINK! Graphic design is traditionally about visual relationships connecting ideas, through words and pictures in order to articulate consumer needs. Often, the commercial designer's job is to select and fit material together in the most appropriate, or visually provocative way, to communicate ideas and sell things, rather than to invite interaction. The ultimate aim is to get the design messages across, and to put a personal stamp on the work. It is a task that should invite activity, not passivity, from the audience.

Profile: Sean O'Mara
Born Netherlands 1967. BA Graphic Design (First Class), 1985-1990 Dunlaoghaire College of Art and Design, Dublin. Established Xon Corp Design Studio, Dublin 1990. MA Graphic Design (Distinction), 1991-1993 Central St. Martins College of Art and Design, London. Senior Designer for Imagination Ltd., London 1993-1995. Currently a Senior Designer/Manager for The Body Shop International, London.

"Design as Input"   Makoto Orisaki

I guess that limitations on the use of color mostly arise from low budgets. In practice I try to prevent this being a limitation on creativity by moving beyond design as pattern and color, to use unlikely materials and processes such as perforating or embossing that don't involve printing. Working this way, everything hangs on getting hold of materials, finding the right techniques, developing an understanding with technical people working in different fields, and keeping on top of costs — all outside the usual orbit of graphic design, but essential for my work. The result is that I can try out new ideas, keeping within a tight budget, and interact with people designers never usually come across.

In recent years I have been working with industrial grade paper such as cardboard, partly out of a desire to test the Japanese sensitivity to the quality and value of paper. Multimedia is currently all the rage, but it can't convey the feel and quality of paper, and here, I think, lies paper's *forte* as a medium. Paper used in Japan for printing is often a bland, standardized quality, dictated by its perceived suitability. I would like to see greater use of different types of paper, including recycled paper, that have more character. Getting involved myself in the development and production of new materials and techniques, I am finding direct mail design an area where I can experiment with these ideas most effectively.

I'm now working on design that uses no color at all because of its advantages in ease of production and subsequent recycling, and because of its artistic potential.

Profile: Makoto Orisaki
Born 1965. "I have no interest in design as self expression. I'm just concerned to minimize what I call 'human error': choices or actions that have some negative impact. Because the act of giving something form and exposing it to society can exert a certain influence on people's values, lifestyles or cultural perceptions, I feel a sense of responsibility. I believe that designing means using one's insights and producing the best possible answer in every respect — one that's functionally effective, people-friendly, environment-friendly, artistic, humorous.....What you then create transcends the individual designer in its significance."

Einleitung

Als Vorwort zu dieser Sammlung präsentieren wir Ihnen die Kommentare von sechs Designern über das Thema "Design mit ein oder zwei Farben". Sie alle teilen die Ansicht, daß eine Beschränkung hinsichtlich des Gebrauchs von Farbe nicht als Hindernis anzusehen ist, sondern als eine Gelegenheit mit reichem Potential an Gestaltungsmöglichkeiten.

"zwei > vier" cyan

cyan arbeitet ausschließlich im kulturellen bereich. in diesen low- und now-budget-projekten erübrigt sich meist die frage nach aufwendiger reprotechnik, lithografie und vierfarbdruck. daher versuchen wir, die möglichkeiten des ein- und zweifarb-druckes auszuschöpfen und mit diesen zu experimentieren. unabhängig davon ist es für uns auch ästhetisch interessant, mit diesen reduzierten mitteln zu arbeiten. auch der ökologische aspekt ist sehr wichtig. auf die einsparung von filmmaterial, druckplatten, chemie etc. und entsprechende papierauswahl legen wir großen wert..... die reizüberflutung mit << perfekt >> reproduzierter und gedruckter << wirklichkeit >> hat sich unserer meinung nach verbraucht. hight-tech-abbil-dungsqualität für die angestellten einer versicherungsgesellschaft in einem glänzen-den werbeprospekt oder die illustrationen zu einem << heile-welt-verheißenden-bausparangebot >> einer großen bank etc. haben die technischen und ästhetischen möglichkeiten zu sehr strapaziert. davon ausgehend suchen wir nach lösungen, die inhaltlich, haptisch und ästhetisch eine einheit bilden und sich nicht nach einma-ligem, kurzem betrachten abnutzen oder auflösen. dazu suchen wir materialien, die weitgehend unnötige chemie ausschließen. die naturpapiere erfordern eine andere bildbearbeitung, da farben anders stehen und wirken. bei der auftragserteilung besprechen wir dies alles mit den auftraggebern, die sich teilweise nur schwer überzeugen lassen. oft wollen sie trotz knappem geld doch etwas buntes und glänzendes. obwohl wir viel erfahrung im mischen und übereinanderdrucken von zwei farben auf naturpapier haben, bleibt es ein spannendes experiment und die far-ben werden erst an der druckmaschine endgültig abgestimmt.

studio-profil: cyan
"die konzeptionellen überlegungen beschreibt cyan selbst als traditionsbezug auf die gestalterische avantgarde der zwanziger und frühen dreißiger jahre. als vorschlag für eine visuelle kultur, in der die erkenntnis- und elebnisfähigkeit des einzelnen eine entwicklungschance haben. [.....] deshalb die sympa-thie für die fotografie, der souveräne umgang mit montage- und überblendungstechniken, daher auch die fähigkeit, die alte bodoni in einem neuen ausdrucksumfeld aufzuschließen, kulturelle widersprüche in ästhetische spannungen zu verwandeln, text, bild und papier zu einem ganzen zu verschmelzen, das sich der fast-food-logik im betrachten widersetzt." dr. j. petruschat in novum 2/94

"Die Botschaft des Kunden durch Farbe kommunizieren" Stoere Binken Design

Wir arbeiten gerne öfters mit nur einer oder zwei Farben. Dies gibt dem Artwork eine ästhetische Reinheit und Abstraktion, die beim Vierfarbdruck oft verlorengeht. Natürlich ist ein weiterer, nicht weniger wichtiger Aspekt der Ein- und Zweifarb-Arbeiten, daß sie dem Kunden eine Menge Geld sparen. Viele Male ist dies der Hauptgrund dafür, mit limitierten Farben zu arbeiten.

Mit zwei Farben zu gestalten, vermittelt totale Kontrolle über die Intensität der Farben. Die Fusion von zwei Farben produziert weit-ere Farben, die wiederum in unzählige Nuancen variiert werden können. Auf diese Weise kann man auch mit Überlagerungen arbeiten, die weniger zweidimensional wirken, Atmosphäre schaf-fen und die Emotionen des Betrachters stimulieren.

Auf diese Weise mit Farbe zu experimentieren, bringt uns näher zu dem, was gutes Design ausmacht: die Botschaft auf eine direkte, ehrliche und profunde Weise zu kommunizieren. Gutes Design heißt nicht, schöne Dinge zu machen, sondern eine graphische Sprache zu schaffen, die den Intentionen des Kunden dient.

Unglücklicherweise hat die Multimedia-Explosion der letzten Zeit den Rahmen für auffallende, rapide wechselnde Vierfarb-Bilder geschaffen, die kaum dafür genutzt werden, die Aufmerksamkeit des Betrachters zu bekommen. Zu oft wird die Botschaft in diesem Prozeß erstickt.

Studio-Profil: Stoere Binken Design
Wir sind ein ziemlich junges Graphik-Design Studio, beheimatet im holländischen Maastricht. Unser Studio besteht aus zwei guten Freunden. Wir begannen sofort nach dem Studium an der Hochschule der Künste in Maastricht. Wir operieren (inter)national und haben eine Vielzahl von Klienten. Unsere Arbeiten reichen von Firmenerscheinungsbildern zu CD-Covers, Zeitschriften, Flugblättern u.a. Wir haben unsere eigenen Ansichten über Design — und darum werden wir von unseren Kunden ausgewählt.

"Das Objekt von zwei Farben" Darin Beaman

Über 60 Prozent aller Projekte am Art Center sind in einer oder zwei Farben. Das liegt an den begrenzten Mitteln im akademischen Umfeld. Manch einer denkt, daß diese Beschränkungen auch das Design limitieren. Wir sehen jedoch jede einzelne Drucksache als eine Gelegenheit, unsere visuellen Ausdrucksmöglichkeiten zu entwickeln und auszuweiten.

Ein gutes Beispiel dafür ist der in diesem Buch gezeigte Ausstellungskatalog für *Objects* (pg.132). Die Auflage und das Budget waren klein, das Thema jedoch hochinteressant; es schien eine einzigartige Lösung zu verlangen. Die Form des Katalogs betont die Absicht, dieses Buches als Objekt zu betrachten. Wir zeigten die Fäden der Bindung und das Bindeleinen, um deren Dinglichkeit als Teil des Buch-Produktionsprozesses zu betonen. Wir nahmen dem Katalog seinen Umschlagdeckel und benutzen Deckpapier für die Textseiten, alles der Strategie fol-gend, das Buch zu "entmaterialisieren". Diese Elemente wurden kombiniert, um eine subtile Verwirrung der Kategorien Buch und Objekt zu schaffen.

Wir sind besonders bei kleineren Projekten dazu verpflichtet, Risiken zu übernehmen und unkonventionelle Optionen für Konzeption und Produktion auszuprobieren. Wir sind allerdings darauf eingeschworen, auf jedes Detail zu achten, wissen wir doch nie, wohin uns das Projekt führt oder welches neue Denken es inspirieren mag.

Studio-Profil: Design Büro für Art Center College of Design
1986 vom Präsidenten David R. Brown gegründet, ist das Art Center Design Büro verantwortlich für alle Drucksachen des Colleges, Stuart Frolick, Vizepräsident und Creative Director steht dem Büro seit 1987 vor. Der Designer Darin Beaman kam 1991 zum Art Center. Die hier gezeigten Arbeiten wurden über eine Fünf-Jahres-Periode von zwei Art Directoren, fünf Designern und einer kleinen Produktionsmannschaft fertiggestellt.

"Verrücktes tun" Sean O'Mara

Meine Ideen darüber, wie man Persönlichkeit in das Modell der kommerziellen Gestaltung bringt, wurden auf den Kopf gestellt, als ich Semiotik, die Theorie der Zeichen, studierte. Ich fand, daß der Kontext mehr als alles andere Bedeutung und Interpretation definiert. Durch den Gebrauch der graphischen Sprache der Alltagsformen (Fundsachen/Papiere/ Bilder) in vollkommen neuem visuellen Kontext ergab sich ein Weg, verrückte, vertraute Botschaften zu machen — und persönliche Besessenheit in die Gestaltungsarbeit einzubringen.

In diesem Buch gibt es einige meiner Designs, die mit Kontext spielen und versuchen, durch den Gebrauch einer vertrauten Sprache unvertraute Bedeutungen zu transportieren. Letztendlich will ich den Betrachter, der diese Mehrdeutigkeit nicht erwartet haben mag, zu einer Reaktion provozieren.

Der Diskurs der kommerziellen Sättigung wird benutzt, so hoffe ich, um die Betrachter anzuregen, genauer hinzuschauen und zu DENKEN. Beim Graphik-Design geht es traditionell um visuelle Beziehungen, um die Verbindung von Worten und Bildern, darum die Bedürfnisse der Kunden zu artikulieren. Oft ist es die Aufgabe des Graphik-Designers, Material auszuwählen und zusammenzufügen, auf die ansprechendste Art oder auf visuell provozierende Weise. Damit sollen Ideen kommuniziert und Dinge verkauft werden, mehr als um zu Interaktion einzuladen. Das letztendliche Ziel ist es, die Design-Botschaft hinüberzubringen und der Arbeit einen persönlichen Stempel aufzudrücken. Es ist eine Aufgabe, die das Publikum zu Aktivität einladen sollte, nicht zur Passivität.

Profil: Sean O'Mara
Geboren in Holland 1967. Ausbildung in Graphik-Design am Dunlaoghaire College of Art and Design, Dublin, 1985-1990. Gründung des Xon Corp Design Studio, Dublin, 1990. Weiterbildung im Graphik-Design am Central St. Martins College of Art and Design, London, 1991-1993. Leitender Designer bei Imagination Ltd., London, 1993-1995. Heute Leitender Designer für The Body Shop International, London.

"Design als Input" Makoto Orisaki

Vermutlich kommen Beschränkungen im Gebrauch von Farben durch Budgetrestriktionen. Ich versuche, dies nicht zu einer Limitierung der Kreativität werden zu lassen. Design sehe ich nicht nur als Textur und Farbe, ich verwende auch besondere Materialien und außergewöhnliche Bearbeitungsverfahren wie Perforation, Stanzung und Prägung. Um die Kosten niedrig zu halten, hängt bei dieser Arbeitsweise alles davon ab, das richtige Material und die richtigen Techniken zu finden. Das geht oft über den üblichen Horizont des Graphik-Design hinaus, aber ohne dem geht es für mich nicht. Ich kann so neue Ideen ausprobieren und auch mit Leuten interagieren, mit denen ich sonst kaum in Kontakt käme.

In den letzten Jahren arbeite ich mit Industriepapieren wie z. B. solches für Verpackungen, auch um die Sensitivität der Japaner hinsichtlich Qualität und Wert von Papier zu testen. Multimedia ist heute das Schlagwort. Damit kann man aber nicht das Gefühl von Papier vermitteln - und darin liegt ja gerade die Stärke des Papiers als Medium. Meist wird in Japan standardisiertes Druckpapier verwandt, bestimmt durch seine jeweilige Eignung für das Druckverfahren. Ich selbst würde gerne intensiveren Gebrauch verschiedener Papiertypen sehen, einschließlich dem von Recyclingpapier. Diese Papiere sind charaktervoller. Am effektivsten kann ich bei Direct Mailings auf die Entwicklung und die Produktion neuer Materialien einwirken.

Kürzlich habe ich mit Designs begonnen, die überhaupt keine Farbe mehr brauchen. Das vereinfacht die Produktion und das Recycling - und eröffnet ein neues künstlerisches Potential.

Profil: Makoto Orisaki
Geboren 1965 "Ich habe überhaupt kein Interesse an Design als Mittel der Selbstdarstellung. Ich versuche, das was ich 'menschliche Fehler' nenne, zu minimieren: Entscheidungen oder Aktionen mit negativem Einfluß. Weil der Formgebungsakt und die Konfrontationen der Gesellschaft mit der Arbeit einen Einfluß auf die Werte der Leute, ihren Lebensstil oder ihre kulturelle Aufnahme ausübt, habe ich ein Gefühl der Verantwortlichkeit. Für mich ist das Gestalten der Gebrauch von Einsichten und die Darstellung der bestmöglichen, positiven Antwort in jeder Hinsicht - eine, die hinsichtlich ihrer Funktion effektiv ist, menschenfreundlich, umweltfreundlich, künstlerisch, humorvoll und so weiter. Was man dann schafft, transzendiert den individuellen Designer in seiner Bedeutung."

"Erinnerungen an Farbe" Jean-Benoît Lévy

Was ist Ihre Lieblingsfarbe, Sie, der Sie diesen Text lesen? Bei mir persönlich wechselt sie, je nach Stimmung und manchmal auch nach Jahreszeit.

Bei Nacht, bei Tag und bei den verschiedenen Lichtarten ist Farbe ständig in Konfrontation mit ihrer Umgebung. Genau wie Photographie und Typographie ist die Auswahl der Farben essentiell. Farben existieren durch die Gefühle, die sie erzeugen. Sobald diese determiniert sind, ist die Frage nicht mehr "Wie viele Farben?" sondern "Welche Farben?"

Im Falle der Serie von Theaterplakaten, die ich für Basel schuf, las ich erst die Stücke bevor ich anfing, so daß mein Design mit dem aufgeführten Stück korrespondieren konnte. Ich fand, daß Autoren ihre Texte oft damit beginnen, spezifische Plätze (eine Stadt, ein Wald), eine Tageszeit (Morgen, Abend) oder eine Umgebung (im Haus, im Freien) vorzustellen, die dann auf eine oder mehrere Farben anspielen.

Ich erlaube mir auch, mich durch das, was ich um mich herum sehe, beeinflussen zu lassen: Mode, andere Graphik-Designs, innovative Flyer, verwobene Kombinationen in der Natur und sogar durch Zufälligkeiten, wie beim Auswaschen meiner Pinsel. Bewußt über die Wichtigkeit solcher "visuellen Momente", versuche ich sie in meinem "Farbgedächtnis" zu halten.

Nachdem eine künstlerische Richtung eingeschlagen ist, entwickeln sich Farben kontinuierlich weiter, sogar bis hin zur Produktion. Es ist beim Drucker an der Druckmaschine, wo die letzten Entscheidungen über Ton, Transparenz, Tiefe und Sättigung gefällt werden. Und später, wenn ich das Plakat in den Strassen hängen sehe, kann ich letztendlich sehen, ob die Farbentscheidungen die richtigen waren.

Welche Farben werden Sie heute tragen? Wählen Sie sie gut, denn sie werden auch ein Spiegel Ihrer Persönlichkeit sein !

Profil: Jean-Benoît Lévy
Geboren 1959. 1978-1983 Vorkurs und anschliessend die Grafikfachklasse der Schule für Gestaltung in Basel. 1983-1986 Grafiker für die Schweizer Mustermesse. Sommer 1987 Presse-Grafiker in Lausanne für zwei Magazine. 1987 ein halbes Jahr in San-Francisco, als Freelancer. Zurück in Basel eröffnete er im Sommer 1988 sein eigenes Atelier "And, Trafic Grafic". 1991-1996 unterrichtete er einmal wöchentlich am "Art Center College of Design Europe". 1993-1994 war er ebenso in der Schule für Gestaltung in Basel. Im Winter 1995-1996 für Wintersession in der "RISD" (Rhode Island School of Design) in Providence, USA, als Gastdozent tätig. Seine Tätigkeit umfasst das ganze Spektrum zwischen Grafik und Werbung. Er hat gerade eine Briefmarke für die Schweizer PTT realisiert.

editorial notes

Credit Format クレジットフォーマット

Creative Staff 制作スタッフ
CD: Creative director
AD: Art director
D: Designer
P: Photographer
I: Illustrator
CW: Copywriter
PD: Producer
DF: Design firm
A: Agency
CL: Client
Country from which submitted 国名
Year of completion 制作年

カラーサンプルについて

本書は4色のプロセスカラーで印刷されています。参考資料として
各クレジットの端にカラーサンプルを掲載しましたが、実際の作品の
色とは多少異なるものもあることをあらかじめご了承ください。
(カラーサンプルは各作品提供者からの情報をもとにしていますが、情報が不
足している一部作品については小社で色を判断しました。)
また蛍光色・メタリックカラーについては下記記号で表記しました。
F = (Fluorescent ink)　蛍光色
M = (Metallic ink)　　メタリックカラー

Color Samples

This book has been printed using the standard 4-color printing process. The credit
details include color samples given for reference purposes, which may vary slightly
from the actual color of the
artwork due to the printing process.

The color samples are based on information
received from our contributors.
In a small number of cases where the information was insufficient,
the editors have made their own judgement.

Abbreviations are used to indicate special inks as follows:
F = fluorescent ink
M = metallic ink

提供者の意向により、クレジットデータの一部に
掲載していないものがあります。

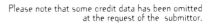
Please note that some credit data has been omitted
at the request of the submittor.

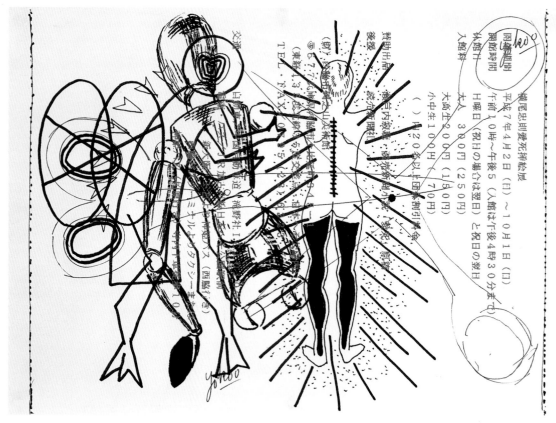

1. D: Daniela Haufe / Detlef Fiedler DF: Cyan CL: Bauhaus Dessau Germany 1995 F

2. AD, D, I: Tadanori Yokoo CL: Okanoyama Museum of Art Japan 1995

D: Daniela Haufe / Detlef Fiedler **DF:** Cyan **CL:** Form + Zweck Germany 1994

AD: U-cef Hanjani **D:** Martin Venezky **P:** Robert Olding **CW:** Bob Rickert **A:** J. Walter Thompson San Francisco
CL: San Francisco AIDS Foundation - Needle Exchange USA 1996

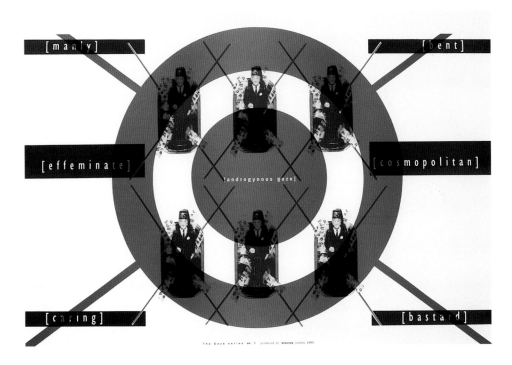

1. CD, D: Seán O'Mara P: Teelesh Bisnauthsing DF, CL: Xon Corp   UK 1993

2. CD, D, P: Seán O'Mara DF: Xon Corp CL: Turning Point UK 1991 F

劇団山の手事情社公演「ドリフタース」

劇団山の手事情社 実験公演
「即興としての演劇」

1. AD, D: Osamu Fukushima CL: Yamanote Jijohsha   Japan 1996

2. AD, D: Osamu Fukushima CL: Yamanote Jijohsha   Japan 1996

新潮ミステリー倶楽部

新潮ミステリー倶楽部

新潮ミステリー倶楽部

AD, D, I: Gugi Akiyama CL: Shinchosha Japan 1994

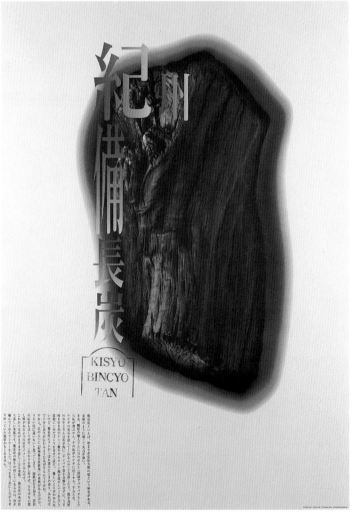

CD, AD, D: Kisei Oka P: Tsukasa Horie CW: Kazuhiko Kamiyama CL: Creative Studio Beans   Japan 1995
＊Heat-stamped 焼き印

AD: Yukio Ikoma D: Yumiko Kawasaki P: Yasuto Okumura CL: JAGDA Japan 1995

1, 2, 4 CD, AD, D: Jean-Benoît Lévy P: Stefan Meichtry Silkscreen: Albin Uldry DF: AND (Trafic Grafic)
CL: Theater Marat - Sade Switzerland 1. 1995 / 2. 1993 / 4. 1992

3 CD, AD, D: Jean-Benoît Lévy P: Martin Klotz Silkscreen: Albin Uldry DF: AND (Trafic Grafic) CL: Theater Marat - Sade Switzerland 1996

CD, AD, D: Jean-Benoît Lévy P: Stefan Meichtry Silkscreen: Albin Uldry DF: AND (Trafic Grafic) CL: Theater Marat - Sade Switzerland 1993

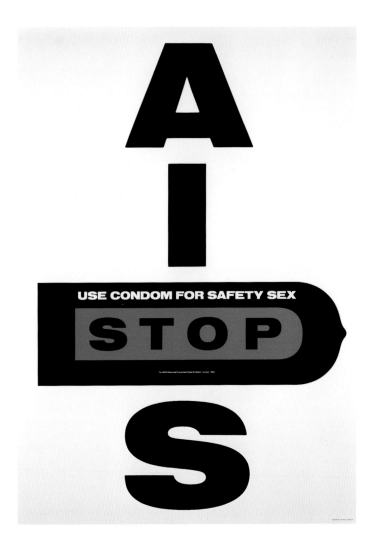

1. AD, D: Yusaku Tomoeda CL: JAGDA Japan 1993

2. AD, D: Yusaku Tomoeda CL: JAGDA Japan 1995

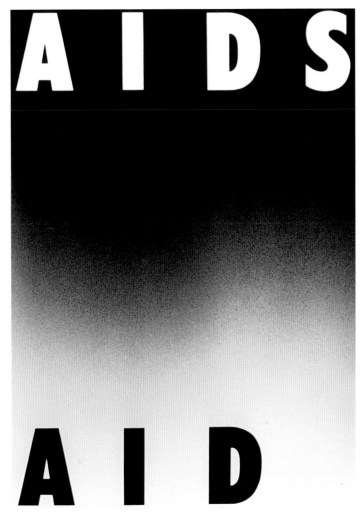

1. **AD, D**: Koichi Sato **CL**: Tokyo Art Directors Club   Japan 1993

2. **AD, D**: Koichi Sato **CL**: Tokyo Art Directors Club   Japan 1993

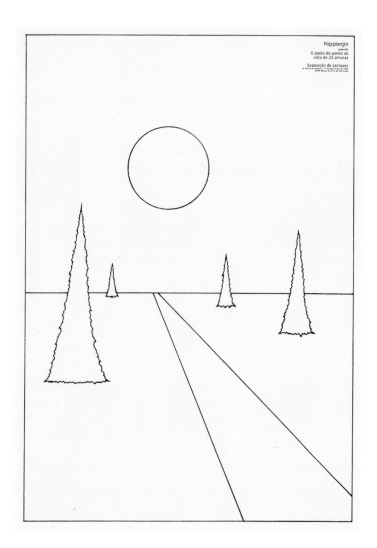

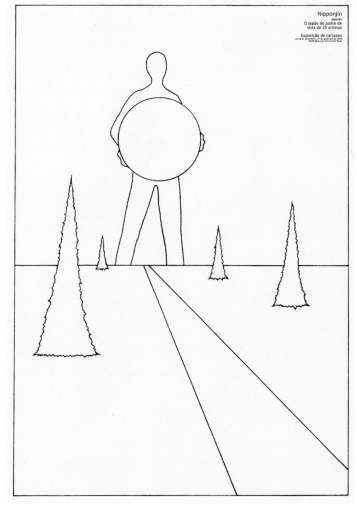

AD, I: Keiji Ito **Coordinator**: Takako Terunuma **DF**: Lop Lop Design **CL**: MASP   Japan   1996

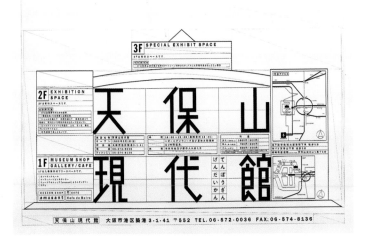

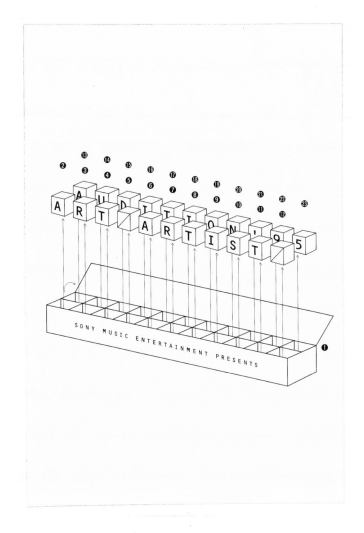

1. AD, D: Norio Nakamura CL: Tempozan Contemporary Museum Japan 1996
＊Varnish

2. AD: Norio Nakamura D: Hiromi Watanabe CL: Sony Music Entertainment (Japan) Inc. Japan 1995
＊Varnish

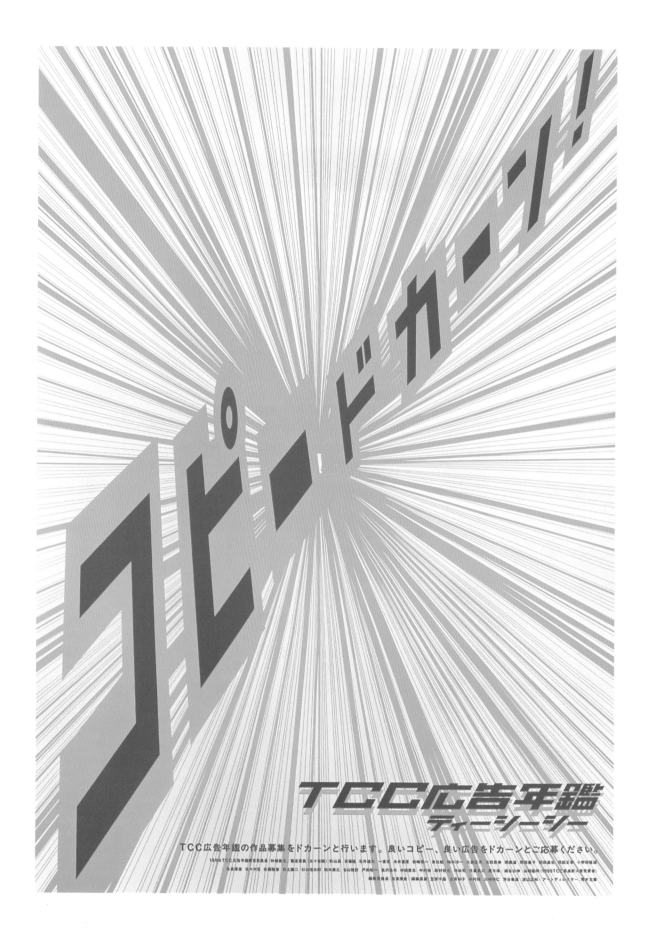

CD: Yasuhiko Sakura AD, D: Katsunori Aoki D: Seijiro Kubo DF: Sun-Ad Co., Ltd. CL: Seibundo Shinkosha Japan 1996

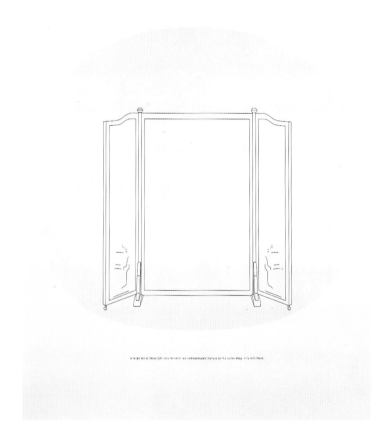

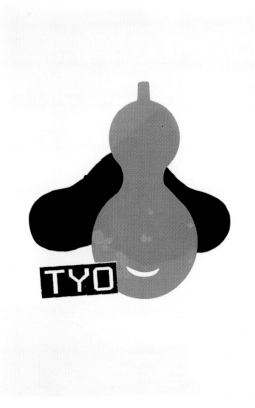

1, 2 **AD, D, I**: Katsunori Aoki Japan 1992

3, 4 **AD, D, I**: Katsunori Aoki Japan 1995

1. **AD, D, CL:** Kozue Takechi Japan 1995

2. **AD, D, CL:** Kozue Takechi Japan 1994

1. **AD, D:** Akio Okumura **DF:** Packaging Create Inc. **CL:** New Oji Paper Co., Ltd. Japan 1996

2. **AD:** Akio Okumura **D:** Mitsuo Ueno **P:** Nob Fukuda **DF:** Packaging Create Inc. **CL:** New Oji Paper Co., Ltd. Japan 1996

D: Daniela Haufe / Detlef Fiedler DF: Cyan CL: Bauhaus Dessau Germany 1994-1996

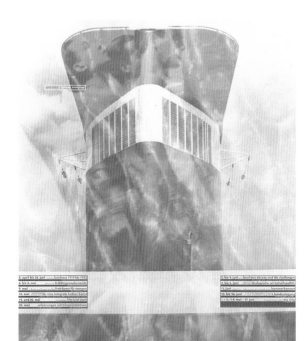

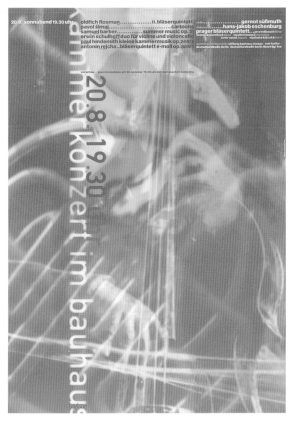

D: Daniela Haufe / Detlef Fiedler   DF: Cyan   CL: Bauhaus Dessau   Germany   1994-1996

D: Daniela Haufe / Detlef Fiedler DF: Cyan CL: Bauhaus Dessau   Germany   1994-1996

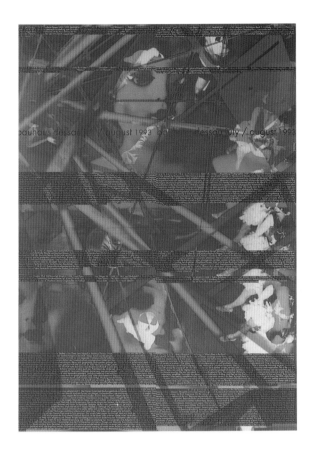

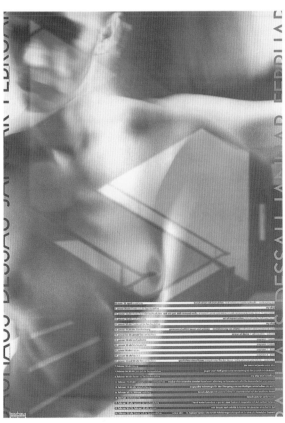

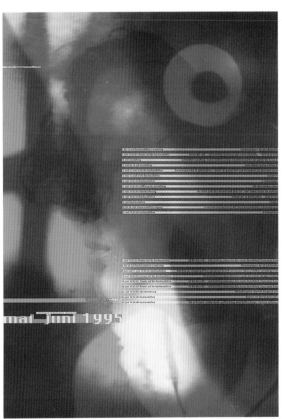

D: Daniela Haufe / Detlef Fiedler DF: Cyan CL: Bauhaus Dessau Germany 1994-1996

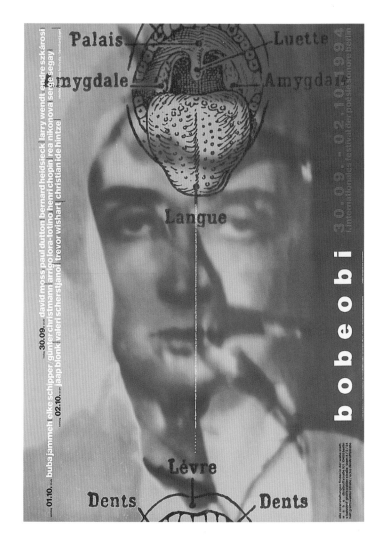

1. D: Daniela Haufe / Detlef Fiedler DF: Cyan CL: Kampagne Gegen Wehrdflicht Germany 1991 *Anti-war poster

2. D: Daniela Haufe / Detlef Fiedler DF: Cyan CL: Förderband E. V. Germany 1994

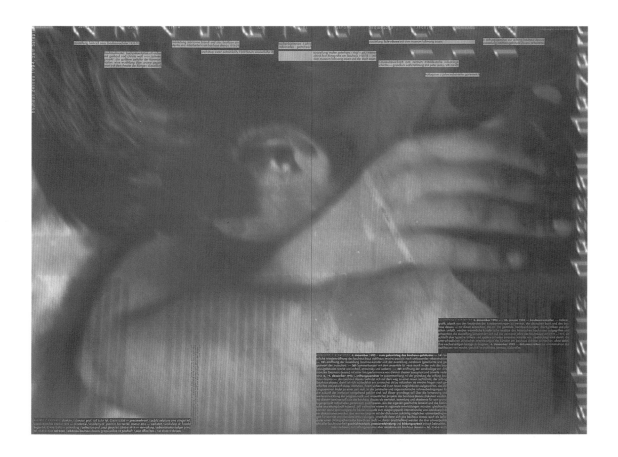

1. D: Daniela Haufe / Detlef Fiedler DF: Cyan CL: Bauhaus Dessau Germany 1994-1996

2. D, P: Daniela Haufe D: Detlef Fiedler DF: Cyan CL: Kammeroper Berlin Germany 1995

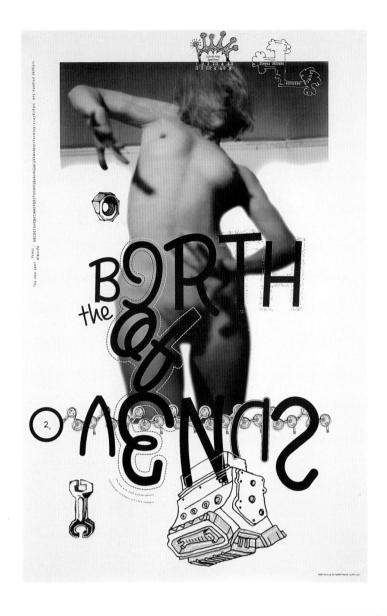

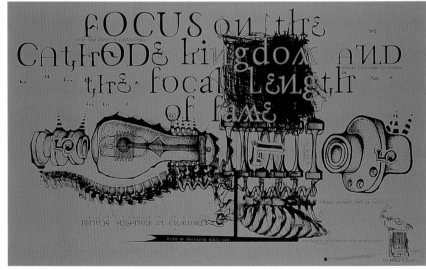

1. CD, P, I: Elliott Peter Earls CL: The Apollo Program   USA   F ▮

2. CD, P, I: Elliott Peter Earls CL: The Apollo Program   USA

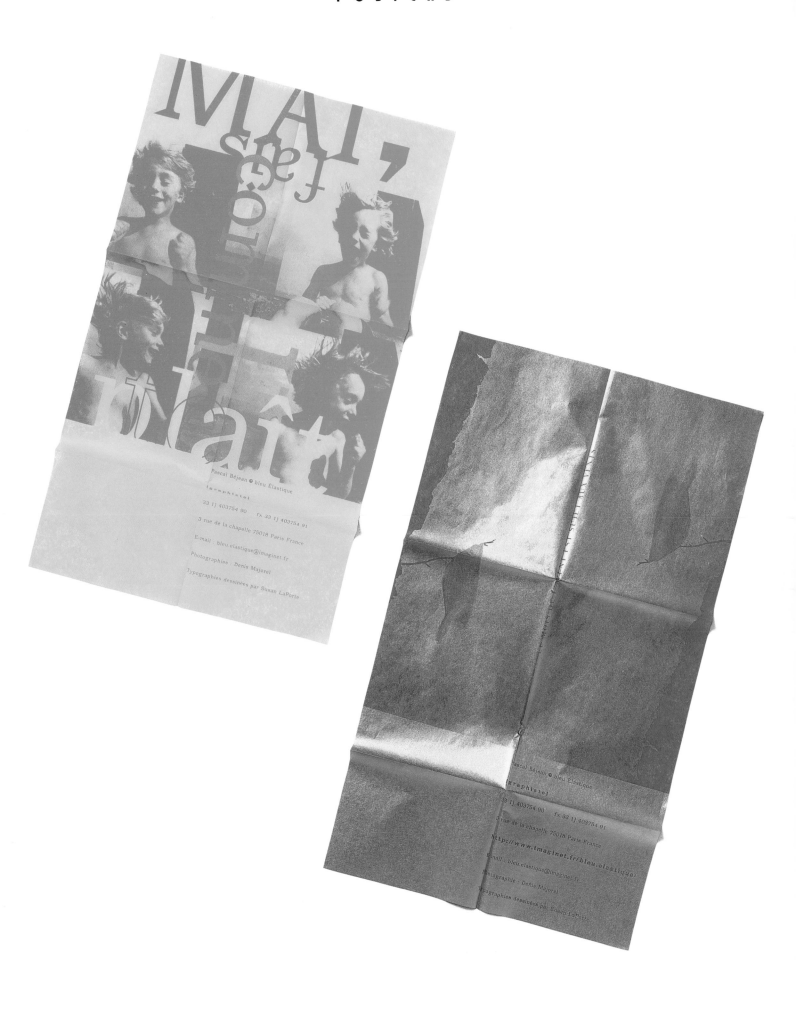

F M CD, AD, D: Pascal Béjean P: Denis Majorel DF, CL: Bleu Élastique France 1996

1. **CD, AD, D:** Silvana Mattievich **CL:** Centro Cultural Banco do Brasil   Brazil   1996

 2. **AD, D:** Emanuel Barbosa **DF:** Emanuel Barbosa Design **CL:** Câmara Municipal do Porto   Portugal   1995

M ▮ 1. CD, AD, D, I: Sonia Greteman D: James Strange CL: Connect Care AIDS Program   USA   1995

2. CD, AD, D, I: Don Weller DF: The Weller Institute for the Cure of Design, Inc. CL: Park City Performances   USA   1994

1. CD, AD, D: Carlos Segura DF: Segura Inc. CL: Elements USA 1996

2. CD, AD, D, I: John Sayles DF: Sayles Graphic Design CL: American Institute of Architects USA 1996   F

1. CD: Dana Arnett AD: Curt Schreiber D: Ken Fox DF: VSA Partners, Inc. CL: Harley - Davidson   USA 1992

F 2. AD, D: Hiromi Watanabe I: Iruka Ikaruga CL: Sony Music Entertainment (Japan) Inc. / Sony Magazines   Japan 1996

1. CD: Masahide Norikuni D: Chieko Maenishi DF: Sankyo Agency Co., Ltd. CL: Sun TV Japan 1995

2. AD: Dana Arnett D: Curt Schreiber DF: VSA Partners CL: Harley Davidson Motor Co. USA 1994

1. CD, AD, D, I: Bjorn Akselsen **Computer Art**: Pattie Belle Hastings DF: Icehouse Design CL: The Atlanta College of Art USA 1993

2. CD, AD: Sonia Greteman AD, D: James Strange CL: Piping & Equipment USA 1996

1. **D, Sculptor:** Daniel R. Smith **P:** Sean Bolan **DF:** Command Z **CL:** Fenix   USA 1996

2. **CD, AD, D:** Michel Bouvet **P:** Francis Laharrague **CL:** Maison des Arts, Créteil France 1992

CD, AD: Stefan Sagmeister D: Veronica Oh DF: Sagmeister Inc. CL: Energy Records USA 1995

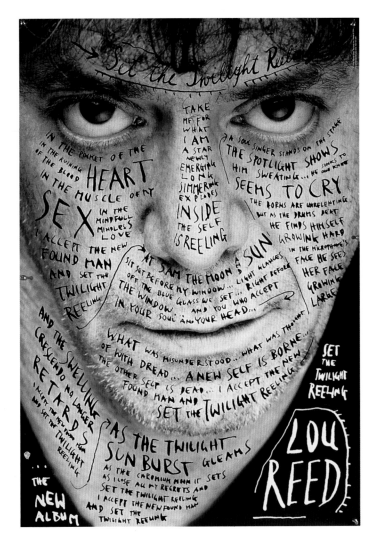

1. **CD, AD, D, DF:** Ralph Schraivogel **Printer:** Albin Uldry **CL:** Zurich Film Podium Switzerland 1996

2. **CD, AD, D:** Stefan Sagmeister **P:** Timothy Greenfield Sanders **DF:** Sagmeister Inc. **CL:** Warner Brothers USA 1996

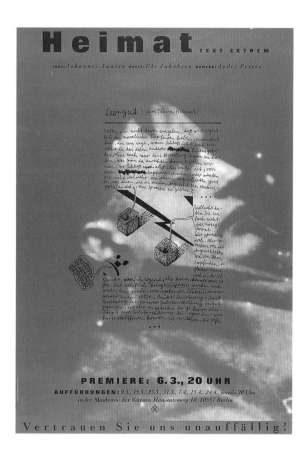

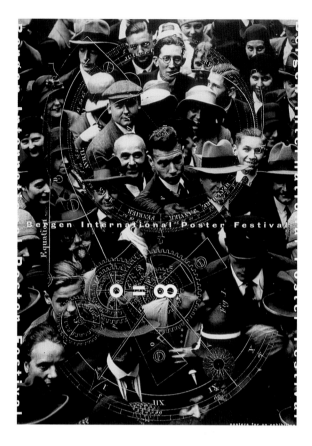

1. CD, AD, D: Ute Zscharnt I: Johanna Jansen CL: Akademic der Künste   Germany

2. CD, AD, D: Dieter Feseke P: Xanti Schawinski (Bauhaus) DF: Grappa Design CL: Angon Jonnsen & Bernt   Germany 1993

3. CD, AD, D: Dieter Feseke P, CL: Stiftung Bauhaus Dessau DF: Grappa Design   Germany 1995

4. CD, AD, D, P, I: Andreas Trogisch / Dieter Feseke CL: Berliner Film Kunsthaus Germany 1992

5. CD, AD, D, P: Heike Grebin / Andreas Trogisch DF: Grappa Design CL: Bergen Poster Festival Germany 1993

6. CD, AD, D, P: Heike Grebin / Andreas Trogisch DF: Grappa Design CL: Filmmuseum Potsdam Germany 1995

1. CD, AD, D: Tadeusz Piechura DF: Atelier Tadeusz Piechura CL: W. D. K. - Kalisz Poland 1995

2. AD, D: Norio Kudo P: Takahito Sato DF: Magna Inc. Advertising CL: JAGDA Japan 1995

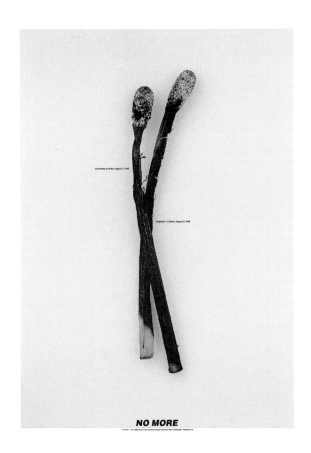

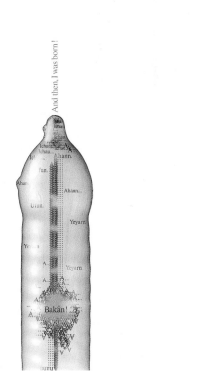

3. **AD, D, I:** Norio Nakamura **CL:** Gallery Preview Japan 1995

4. **CD:** Yoshifumi Shibukawa **AD:** Keisuke Kimura **D:** Maki Yanagishima **P:** Kyoko Harada **CL:** Toyo Information Systems Co., Ltd. Japan 1996

5. **AD:** Keisuke Kimura **D:** Maki Yanagishima **P:** Naohiro Isshiki **CL:** Rakuten Design Room Japan 1996

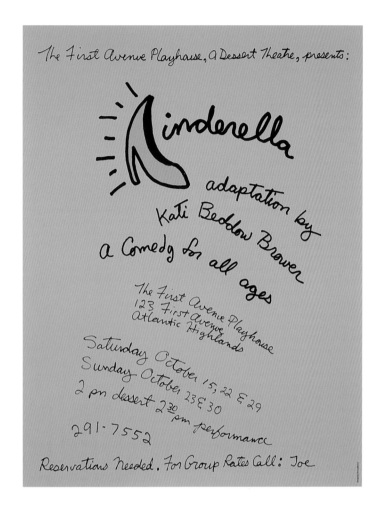

1. AD, D, I: Steven Brower DF: Steven Brower Design CL: First Avenue Play House   USA 1994
∗ Varnish

2. AD, D, I: Steven Brower DF: Steven Brower Design CL: The Looking Glass Theatre   USA 1994

1. D: Kees Wagenaars P: M. Verhoeven DF: Case CL: Teater '77 Netherlands 1995

2. D: Kess Wagenaars DF: Case CL: Teater '77 Netherlands 1994

3. D: Kees Wagenaars I: Sieb DF: Case CL: Zaal 16 Netherlands 1996

shiseido beautysaloon

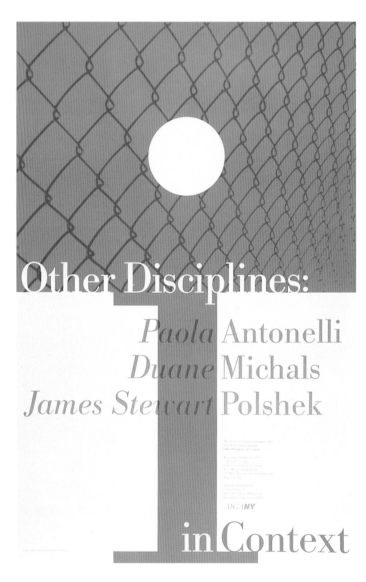

Other Disciplines:
Paola Antonelli
Duane Michals
James Stewart Polshek

in Context

1. CD: Aoshi Kudo AD, D, I: Keiko Hirano CL: Shiseido Beauty Saloon Shibuya Japan 1994

2. AD, D, P: J. Graham Hanson DF: J. Graham Hanson Design CL: American Institute of Graphic Arts / New York USA 1995

1, 2. CD: Hiroyoshi Hidaka AD, D: Eiichi Sakota D, I: Toshio Kawakami DF: Rec 2nd CL: Hidaka Office   Japan   1994

3. AD, D, I: Kari Piippo DF: Kari Piippo OY CL: Volks Theater Rostock   Finland   1996

4. CD, AD, D: Michel Bouvet CL: Amnesty International   France   1993

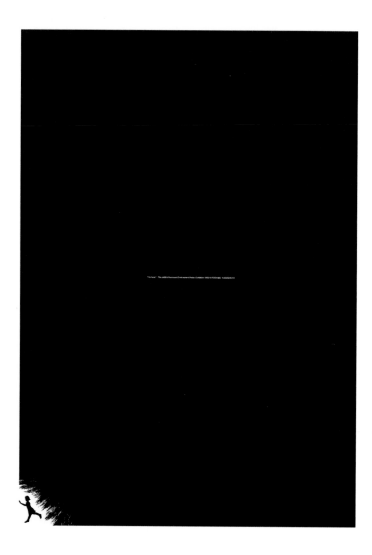

1. AD, D, I: Gugi Akiyama CL: JAGDA Japan 1995

2. AD, D, I: Katsunori Aoki CL: HB Gallery Japan 1993

1. CD, AD, D, P, I: John Sayles CW: Wendy Lyons DF: Sayles Graphic Design CL: Continuum Healthcare USA 1996

2. CD, AD, D, I: John Sayles D: Jennifer Elliott CW: Jack Jordison DF: Sayles Graphic Design CL: IMT USA 1996

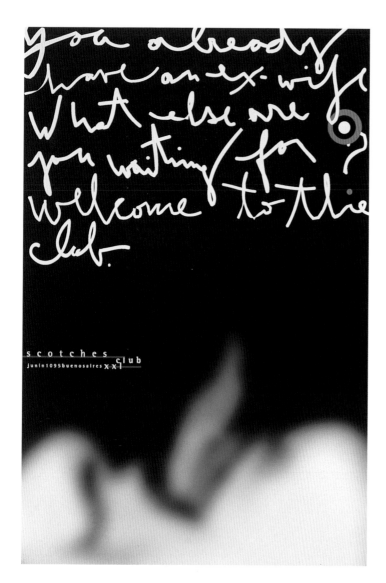

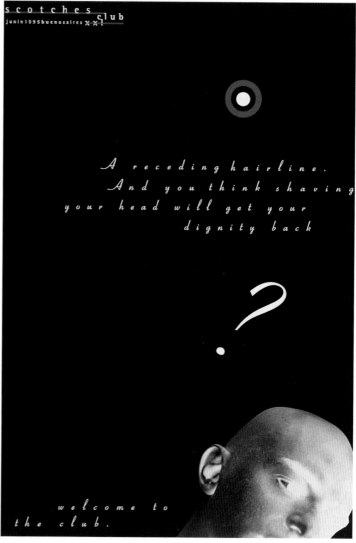

CD: Silvio Panizza AD, D, P: Marcela Augustowsky P: Guillermo Vega CW: Fernanda Cava DF: Pandora's Box CL: Club XXI Argentina 1994

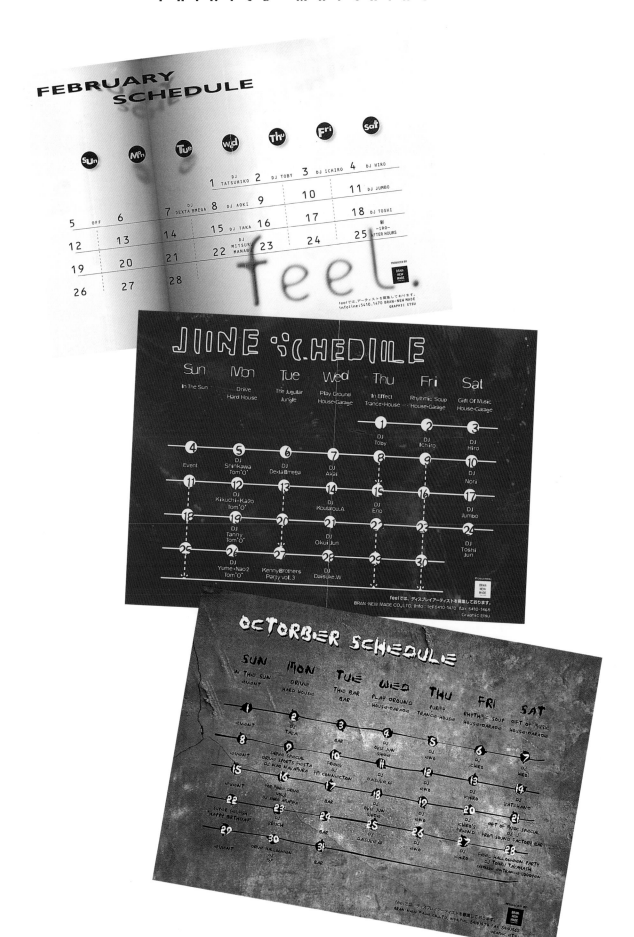

1. D, CL: Tsumori Chisato Japan 1996   M

2. CD, AD: Cinema Cats D: Masaharu Suzuki CL: Comstock Japan

1, 3, 4. CD, AD, D: Makoto Orisaki CL: E & Y Co., Ltd. Japan 1995-1996
*4. Perforated ミシン目

2. CD, AD, D: Makoto Orisaki I: Michael Young CL: E & Y Co., Ltd. Japan 1995

MONSIEUR NICOLE

B Y
Y U K I O
KOBAYASHI

ROBERT JEFFERSON / Broadcast Journalist

AD: Hisao Sugiura D, DF: Studio Super Compass P: Naoaki Matsumoto CL: Nicole Co., Ltd.   Japan 1996

1. CD: Troy Bailly D: Kathryn Lissack DF: Prototype Design CL: Arts Undergraduate Society of UBC   Canada   1996

2. D: Troy Bailly / Stephen Parkes DF: Prototype Design CL: The Red Lounge   Canada   1996

3. D: Stephen Parkes DF: Prototype Design CL: Starfish Room   Canada   1994

teater '77 - vr 10 en za 11 mei 1996

Sinds wanneer ben jij geïnteresseerd in wat je slikt?

Maar soms ben ik ook wel gelukkig.

Wat voegt carrière toe aan je menszijn, wat geeft kennis je ?

Het financiële plaatje moet eerst rond.

ogen strooien.

Mensen, laat je

De werking van

dan ooit geda

Seresta, e

KLANTEN
KUNNEN
NIET
WACHTEN

TEEJATERGROEP ORION

Teejatergroep Orion speelt het toneelspel 'Klanten kunnen niet wachten' van de auteur Jan Staal.
Het toneelspel in vier bedrijven gaat over mensen die, vastgeroest in hun dagelijks bestaan, de grote verwachtingen van hun
leven niet verwezenlijkt zien worden.
De auteur Jan Staal zet een bontgeschakeerd gezelschap neer.
Mensen met verschillende achtergronden. De een dromerig, terugdenkend aan de verliefdheid uit haar jeugd, de andere met
verstandsverbijstering door traumatische oorlogservaringen of hij die zich vasthoudt aan de fantasierijke dromen over de
toekomst.
Wanneer er een moment komt in hun leven waarin zij de cirkel van hun getoond zijn kunnen doorbreken, ontbreekt hen de
moed. Ook beseffen zij dat ze niet meer zonder elkaar kunnen leven.

Caspar Willers

ward Albee's

R BANG VOOR
NIA WOOLF?

Teater '77 in de Spiegelzaal
do 16, vr 17, za 18 en zo 19 november
Regie: Paul Terwijn
Aanvang: 20.00 uur, entree fl. 12,50 (cjp/pas 65 fl. 10,-)
Reserveren aanbevolen: 076 - 5145092

1. AD, I: Kees Wagenaars DF: Case CL: Teater '77 Netherlands 1996

2. D: Kees Wagenaars DF: Case CL: Teejatergroep Orion Netherlands 1994

3. D: Kees Wagenaars DF: Case CL: Teater '77 Netherlands 1995

CD, AD, D, I, CW: Andrew Holland / Daniel Holliday DF: Trouble CL: The Sausage Machine UK 1989-1994

65

1. CD: Marcia Romanuck D: Alison Scheel / Fran McKay DF: The Design Company CL: Center for Puppetry Arts   USA   1995-1996

2. D: Kazuo Abe I: Yoko Tanimoto CL: The Room   Japan   1996

3. D, P: Kazuo Abe DF: Rhythmic Garden   Japan   1996

1. CD, AD, D, I, CW: Rvvd Van Empel DF: Van Den Beginne BV CL: Stichting Animatie   Netherlands 1992   M

2. CD, AD, D, I: Troy M. Litten CW: Yolanda Edwards DF: Active White Space CL: 1015 Folsom   USA   1994   F F F

M 1. D: Takao Yamashita Typographer: Simon Taylor CL: Beauty and Beast Japan 1996

2. D: Takao Yamashita CL: Beauty and Beast Japan 1992

3. D: Takao Yamashita P: Schoerner CL: Beauty and Beast Japan 1994

1. CD: Ziggi Golding AD, D: David Calderley CW: Reg Reg CL: Gee Street Records   USA 1995

2. AD, D: Lopetz P: Stek Ag DF: Büro Destruct CL: Kulturfabrik Kofmehl   Switzerland 1996

1. **AD, D:** Sachi Sawada **DF:** "Moss" Design Unit **CL:** Nerd Japan 1996

2. **AD, D:** Lopetz **DF:** Büro Destruct **CL:** ISC Switzerland 1996

3, 4. **AD, D:** Marc Bastard Brunner **DF:** Büro Destruct **CL:** Markthalle Bern Switzerland 1996

1, 3. AD, D: Takayuki Ichige DF: Hal Corporation CL: Ground Level Groove Japan 1996

2. AD, D, Faxcollage: Lopetz DF: Büro Destruct CL: United Tribes Switzerland 1996

4. AD: Yuichi Nakagawa D: Sachiko Kitani DF, CL: Kinema Moon Graphics Japan 1995

1. CD: Mika Kojima / Masanao Takase AD, D, I: Gugi Akiyama CL: G-One., Inc. Japan 1994

2. CD, D: Mikiko Shimizu I: Rieko Mukai CL: Tokyo Can Co., Ltd. Japan 1994

3. CD, D, I: Takumi Iwase AD: Keiji Sugiura DF: Tokyo Guns CL: Club Cover Japan 1996

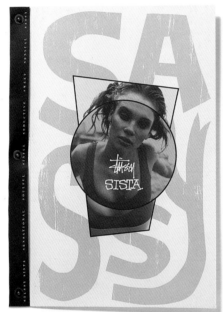

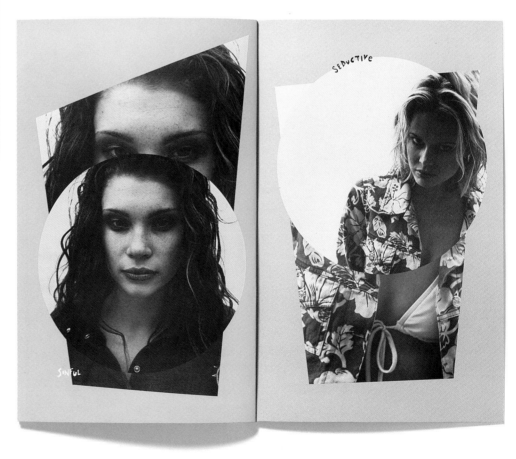

CD, AD, D: Andrew Hoyne DF: Andrew Hoyne Design CL: Stussy Sista   Australia   1995

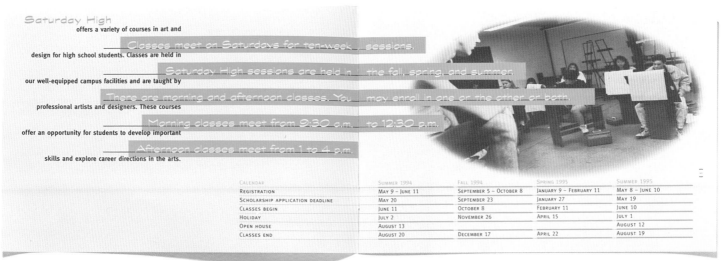

Saturday High offers a variety of courses in art and design for high school students. Classes are held in our well-equipped campus facilities and are taught by professional artists and designers. These courses offer an opportunity for students to develop important skills and explore career directions in the arts.

Classes meet on Saturdays for ten-week sessions. Saturday High sessions are held in the fall, spring, and summer. There are morning and afternoon classes. You may enroll in one or the other or both. Morning classes meet from 9:30 a.m. to 12:30 p.m. Afternoon classes meet from 1 to 4 p.m.

CALENDAR	SUMMER 1994	FALL 1994	SPRING 1995	SUMMER 1995
REGISTRATION	MAY 9 – JUNE 11	SEPTEMBER 5 – OCTOBER 8	JANUARY 9 – FEBRUARY 11	MAY 8 – JUNE 10
SCHOLARSHIP APPLICATION DEADLINE	MAY 20	SEPTEMBER 23	JANUARY 27	MAY 19
CLASSES BEGIN	JUNE 11	OCTOBER 8	FEBRUARY 11	JUNE 10
HOLIDAY	JULY 2	NOVEMBER 26	APRIL 15	JULY 1
OPEN HOUSE	AUGUST 13			AUGUST 12
CLASSES END	AUGUST 20	DECEMBER 17	APRIL 22	AUGUST 19

Classes

You may select one or two of the courses offered. Classes are designed for beginning as well as for more advanced students. Some students take the same course more than once, while others explore many different classes. It's up to you.

Still-life drawing In this class you will learn how to draw three-dimensional objects and increase your knowledge of the effects of light on form, volume, and line. You will work with still-life setups, starting with simple materials and compositions, then move to more complicated media. This is a great class to begin your studies in art or to improve your drawing skills. ESTIMATED COST OF MATERIALS IS $40. CLASSES MEET 9:30 A.M.–12:30 P.M.

Figure drawing Drawing the human figure is important training for all artists. Working with a costumed model, you will develop an understanding of form through increased visual skills. This class offers a good foundation in the basics for beginners as well as for more experienced artists. In class discussions you will learn how artists from the past and present have depicted the figure. ESTIMATED COST OF MATERIALS IS $40. CLASSES MEET 9:30 A.M.–12:30 P.M. OR 1–4 P.M.

Illustration This is a class in which you can apply your drawing skills to illustration projects such as album covers, ads, magazines, or movie posters. Using a variety of media, including graphite, colored pencil, and ink, students will draw from live models as well as from imagination. You will learn about the historical traditions of illustration and about today's illustration styles, as seen in print, film, and video. Some previous study of drawing is recommended. ESTIMATED COST OF MATERIALS IS $40. THIS CLASS IS OFFERED ONLY DURING THE SUMMER SESSION. CLASSES MEET 9:30 A.M.–12:30 P.M.

Painting You will study the basic processes of painting, beginning with studies of light and shadow and working toward complete paintings in a full-color palette. The basic techniques, from preparatory drawing to color mixing, will be covered. For the first day, bring drawing pad and pencils. ESTIMATED ADDITIONAL COST OF MATERIALS IS $90. CLASSES MEET 9:30 A.M.–12:30 P.M.

Basic design A study of the basic elements of design is a foundation for every artist and designer. Through the exploration of different media and collage techniques you will learn about color, line, texture, form, and composition and will be able to apply your understanding to a variety of art and design projects. For the first day, bring an 11" x 19" tracing pad, 2B pencils, a ruler, a triangle, and a note pad. ESTIMATED ADDITIONAL COST OF MATERIALS IS $30. CLASSES MEET 9:30 A.M.–12:30 P.M.

Graphic design Curious about how individuals, companies, and organizations create their "look"? Using the tools of imagery, color, typography, composition, and structure, you will learn to communicate ideas about companies and products. In-class projects enable you to apply your design ideas to projects such as shopping bags, posters, brochures, and logos. ESTIMATED COST OF MATERIALS IS $40. CLASSES MEET 9:30 A.M.–12:30 P.M. OR 1–4 P.M.

Advertising Learn how successful ads are created. You will select a product and create a complete advertising campaign including print ads and television commercials. Your instructor will take you through the steps of producing ads, from concept to layout to designing the type. ESTIMATED COST OF MATERIALS IS $40. CLASSES MEET 1–4 P.M.

Environmental and interior design This course will introduce you to the basic techniques and materials needed to design three-dimensional spaces such as restaurants or parks and give them a unique feeling. Students will be exposed to drafting fundamentals and learn the basics of interior and exterior perspective drawing and model making. Projects may include designing a children's playground and the interior of a coffee house. ESTIMATED COST OF MATERIALS IS $35. CLASSES MEET 9:30 A.M.–12:30 P.M.

Industrial design Industrial designers work on a range of projects, from cassette recorders to cars. This class introduces you to industrial design as a profession and helps you develop some important skills. You will learn about design procedures, production processes, and the marketing of products. ESTIMATED COST OF MATERIALS IS $75. CLASSES MEET 1–4 P.M.

Photography Photography is one of the most compelling of all visual media. This course will review the basics of using a 35mm camera and will involve you in the creative aspects of composition, lighting, and processing. You should know how to use your camera to benefit from this class. Please bring your own camera. Students will not have access to Art Center's laboratory facilities; they may process their work commercially or find their own darkroom facilities. ESTIMATED COST OF MATERIALS IS $15 WEEKLY FOR FILM AND PROCESSING. CLASSES MEET 9:30 A.M.–12:30 P.M.

Film Students will view and critique films and study aspects of the art of filmmaking. They will also have the chance to make several short films or videos. Students may work in video or film, depending on the availability of their own equipment. Students must provide either a Super 8 camera or VHS or 8mm home video camcorder. SUPPLY COSTS WILL BE APPROXIMATELY $20 FOR STUDENTS WORKING IN VIDEO AND $100 FOR THOSE WORKING IN FILM. CLASSES MEET 9:30 A.M.–12:30 P.M.

Materials For all drawing and illustration classes, bring a 20" x 26" drawing board, ten sheets of 17" x 22" white bond paper, an Eagle drafting pencil, 4B and 6B charcoal pencils, a kneaded eraser, and an X-acto knife on the first day. For other classes, bring pencil and paper for taking notes on the first day. Teachers will provide complete information on required materials during the first class meeting. For your convenience there is a Student Store on campus, or you may purchase supplies at any art supply store.

F CD: Stuart I. Frolick D, P: Mike Fink DF, CL: Art Center College of Design USA 1994

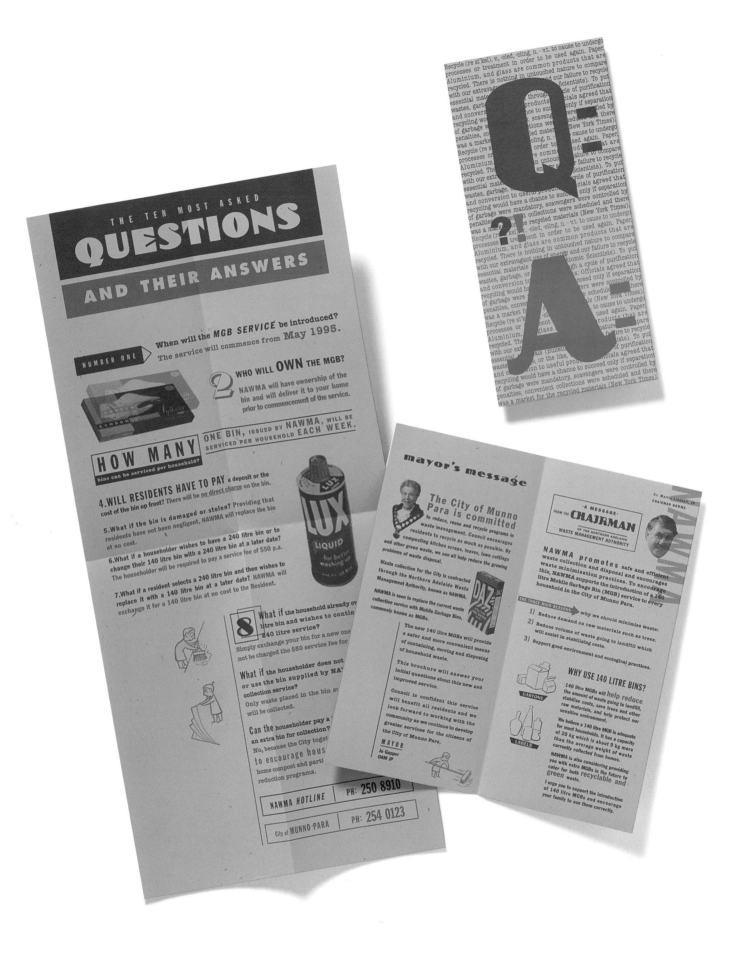

CD, AD: Alexander Musson D: Timothy Murphy DF: Poagi® CL: City of Munno Para   Australia 1994

1. CD, AD: Sonia Greteman AD, D, I: James Strange CL: The Wichita Center for the Arts   USA 1996

2. AD, D: Jack Anderson D: Lisa Cerveny / Jana Wilson / Julie Keenan CW: Jeff Fraga DF: Hornall Anderson Design Works CL: Xact Data Corporation   USA 1995

1. **D:** Daniel R. Smith **DF:** NBBJ Graphic Design **CL:** NBBJ   USA   1996

F

2. **CD:** Stuart I. Frolick **AD:** Darin Beaman **D:** Thomas Muller **P:** Steven A. Heller **DF, CL:** Art Center College of Design   USA   1995

camera nuovo
(new room)

STUDIO

Ralph Mercer is packing up all of his cameras and moving to:

telephone: 617·542·2211
fax: 617·542·1844

RALPH MERCER PHOTOGRAPHY
300 Summer Street, Suite 71
Boston MA 02210

camera obscura
(dark room)

[THE ORIGIN OF PHOTOGRAPHY]

"Close all the shutters and doors until no light enters the camera except through the lens, and opposite hold a sheet of paper, which you move forward and backward until the scene appears in sharpest detail. There on the paper you will see the whole view as it really is, with its distances, its colors and shadows and motion, the clouds, the water twinkling, the birds flying. By holding the paper steady you can trace the whole perspective with a pen, shade it and delicately color it from nature."

from the book Natural Magic by Giovanni
Battista della Porta (1553)

CD, D: Jane Cuthbertson DF: Myriad Inc. P, CL: Ralph Marcer   USA 1995

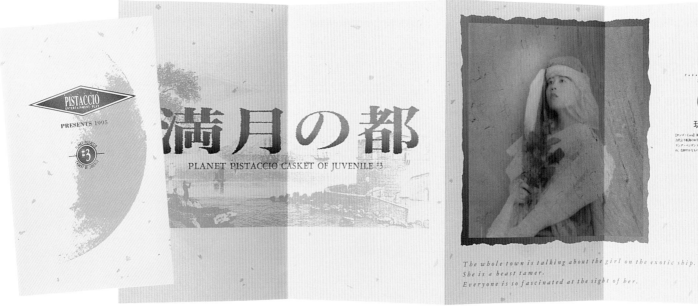

1. PD: Junji Ito CD: Shigeru Yamaoka AD: Keiji Ito D: Yoshiko Okamoto DF: Studio Give / Lop Lop Design Inc.   Japan   1993

2. AD, D: Takeshi Kuroda P: Miwa Isoi DF: Office Sandscape CL: Planet Pistaccio   Japan   1995

3. CD, AD, D, P: Pascal Béjean DF, CL: Bleu Élastique   France   1995

1. AD: Ric Riordon D: Sharon Pece I: Dan Wheaton DF: The Riordon Design Group Inc. CL: Samsung Electronics Canada   Canada 1995

2. CD: Carlos Segura AD, D, I: Laura Alberts DF: Segura Inc. CL: MRSA USA 1996

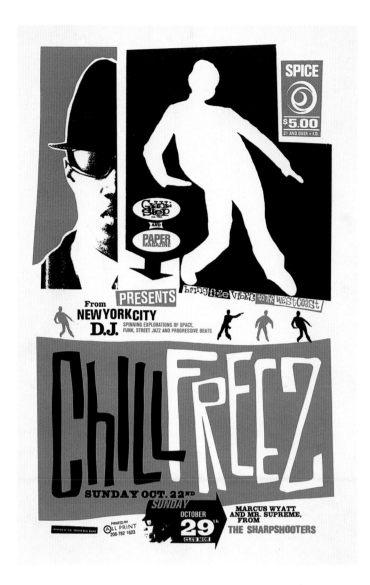

1. AD, D: Yasuhiro Sawada CL: Nippon Paint Co., Ltd.   Japan 1992

M 2. AD, D: Clifford Stoltze D: Wing Ip Ngan Typography: Richard Leighton DF: Stoltze Design CL: Castle von Buhler Records   USA 1996

FALL/WINTER 1996 MATSUDA COLLECTION FOR WOMEN AND MEN BY YUKIO KOBAYASHI

AD, D: Hideki Nakajima CL: Nicole Co., Ltd. Japan 1996

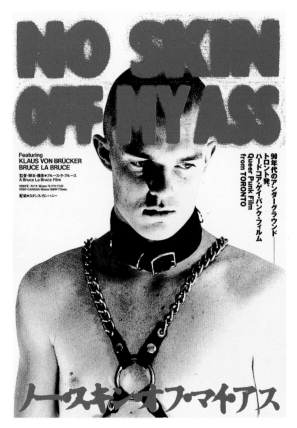

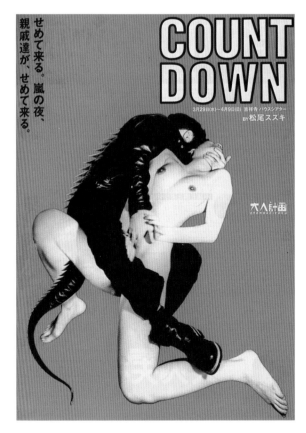

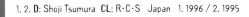

1, 2. D: Shoji Tsumura CL: R·C·S Japan 1. 1996 / 2. 1995

3. CD: Akihiro Suzuki AD, D: Yasunori Arai DF: Picture Disc CL: Stance Company Japan 1992

4. CD: Suzuki Matsuo AD, D: Masami Yoshizawa P: Junsuke Takimoto CL: Otona Keikaku Japan 1995

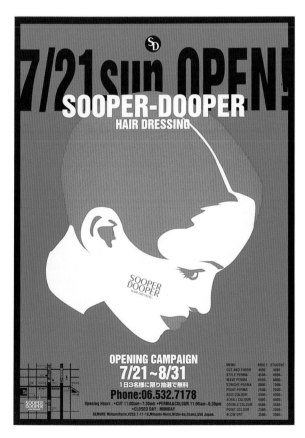

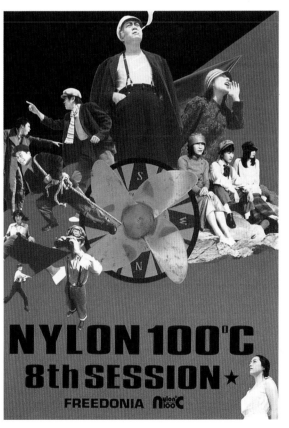

1, 2. CD, AD, D, I: Toru Kunugida DF: Never Land CL: Media Rings Corporation Japan 1992

3. AD, D, I: Sachi Sawada DF: "Moss" Design Unit Japan 1996

4. CD: Keralino Sandrovich AD, D: Masashi Komura D: Chisako Amazutsumi P: Chikako Kamitori CL: Silly Walk Co., Ltd. Japan 1996

1. D, I: Shotaro Manabe CL: Coml Japan 1995

2. CD, D: Peter Grundy CD: Tilly Northedge DF, CL: Grundy & Northedge UK 1995

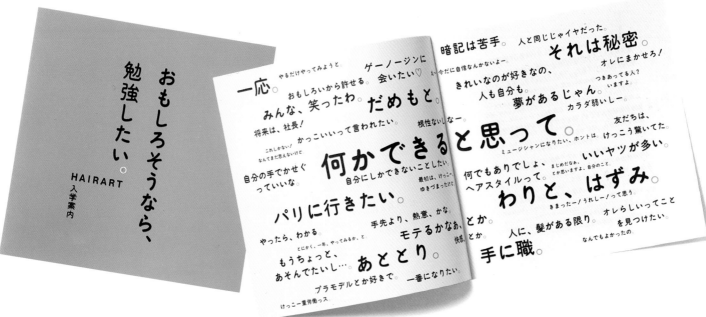

1. CD, AD, D: Hiroaki Konya DF, CL: Kokoku Nojyo Japan 1995

2. CD: Atsuhiro Miyakawa AD, D: Eiichi Sakota CW: Keiko Sato DF: Rec 2nd CL: Hairart Japan 1996

The oFFiCe PaRTy

magazine girls

1. CD, AD: Jim Christie I: Isabelle Dervaux DF, CL: Jim Christie Design USA 1996

2. AD, I: Isabelle Dervaux CL: C. W. C. USA 1996

SEASON'S GREETINGS

1. **AD**: Katsumi Komagata **D**: Aki Ishijima **DF**: One Stroke Co., Ltd. **CL**: Still Waters Japan 1996

2. **AD**: Katsumi Komagata **D**: Aki Ishijima **DF, CL**: One Stroke Co., Ltd. Japan 1995

CD: Suzuki Matsuo AD, D: Masami Yoshizawa P: Junsuke Takimoto I: Yoshiharu Mitsumoto CL: Otona Keikaku   Japan 1996

1. CD: Masaaki Kato AD, D: Eiichi Sakota D: Yoshitaka Shinmori
D, I: Toshio Kawakami DF: Rec 2nd CL: FM Osaka Japan 1996

2. CD, AD, D: Hiroaki Konya DF: Kokoku Nojo CL: Mitsuaki Shibuya Japan 1995

HERRON GALLERY
Indianapolis Center for Contemporary Art
CLAYFEST No. 8
A Juried Biennial of
INDIANA CERAMIC ARTISTS

and

AMACO SELECTS: TEN YEARS OF CERAMIC WORKSHOPS

DECEMBER *5, 1992* - JANUARY *8, 1993*

HERRON SCHOOL OF ART
1701 N. PENNSYLVANIA ST.
INDIANAPOLIS, IN. 46202
317 920-2420

MONDAY - THURSDAY
10:00 AM TO 7:00 PM
FRIDAY 10:00 AM TO 5:00 PM

These exhibitions are funded in part by The Mary Howes Woodsmall Foundation, American Art Clay Co., Inc., the Friends of Herron, the Indiana Arts Commission and the National Endowment for the Arts.

CD, D: Mario A. Mirelez AD, D: Jim Ross DF: Mirelez / Ross Inc. CL: Herron Gallery USA 1992

1. CD, I: Senri Imada AD, D, CL: Sachi Sawada DF: "Moss" Design Unit Japan 1996

2. CD, AD, D: Issay Kitagawa I: Mar Sekiguchi CL: Japan Design Committee Japan 1996

CD, AD, D: Etsu CL: Bran-New Made Co., Ltd. Japan 1995

1. CD: G-Works AD, D, P: Mitsuyuki Odajima CL: Logic Japan 1996

2. AD, D: Akira Sumi CL: Hiroshige Maki Atelier Japan 1996

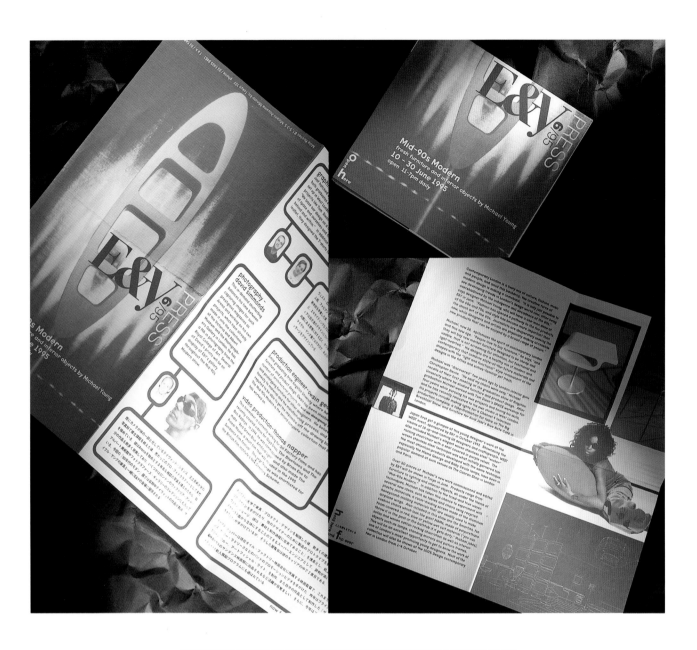

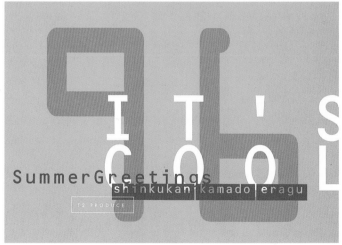

1. **AD, D:** Yasushi Kikuchi **Editor:** Yoichi Nakamuta (E & Y Co., Ltd.) / John Storey **CL:** E & Y Co., Ltd. Japan 1995

2. **AD, D:** Haruki Mori **DF:** Azone + Associates **CL:** T2 Japan 1996

1996.2.9 Wada+guest Gak+Mari

Automatix
info;0333588255

2.23 WAda+PhilFree Sasaki

1. D: Takashi Sasaki CL: Dual Growing System Inc.   Japan 1996

2. CD, AD, D: J. J. F. G. Borrenbergs / R. Verkaart DF: Stoere Binken Design CL: Sirius   Netherlands 1996

3. CD, D: Yasushi Okumura AD: Naoki Kihira CL: Karma   Japan 1995

1. CD, AD, D: Ross McBride DF, CL: Designatorium Japan 1994

2. CD, AD, D, P: Clifford Cheng DF, CL: Voice Design USA 1996

1. **AD:** Charles Shields **D:** Juan Vega **DF, CL:** Shields Design   USA   1993

2. **AD, D:** Haruki Mori **DF:** Azone + Associates   Japan   1996

 1. **AD, D**: Katsunori Aoki **CL**: Peace Card Japan 1995

2. **AD, D**: Katsunori Aoki **I, CL**: Akemi Suetsugu Japan 1994

3. **AD, D**: Katsunori Aoki **CL**: HB Gallery Japan 1996

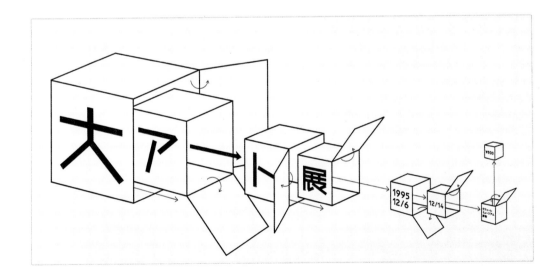

1. CD, D: Keiko Watanabe CL: Tokyo Can Co., Ltd. Japan 1996

2. D, I: Shotaro Manabe CL: Go-Go Project Japan 1996

3. AD: Norio Nakamura D: Hiromi Watanabe CL: Sony Music Entertainment (Japan) Inc. Japan 1995
*Varnish

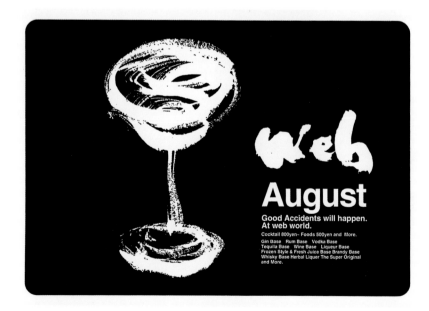

1. CD: Chris H. Sekine AD, D: Noriyoshi Kawahara I: Katsuyuki Nishizuka CL: Yellow Japan 1996

2. CD, AD, D: Hiroaki Doi CL: Uichi Yamamoto Japan 1994

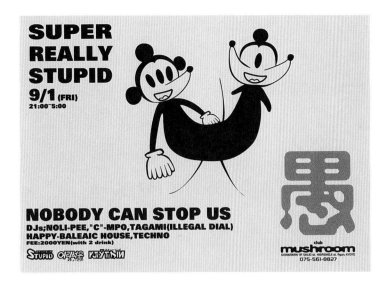

CD: Yukihiko Asano AD, D: Gugi Akiyama P: Takashi Homma Artist: Kazuo Umezu CL: Laforet Harajuku   Japan 1995

1. AD, D, I: Simon Sernec CL: G Klub Slovenia 1991

2. CD, AD, D: André de Castro DF: Interface Designers CL: O Globo Newspaper Brazil

3. AD, D: Kenzo Izutani D: Aki Hirai DF: Kenzo Izutani Office Corp. CL: Parco Japan 1990

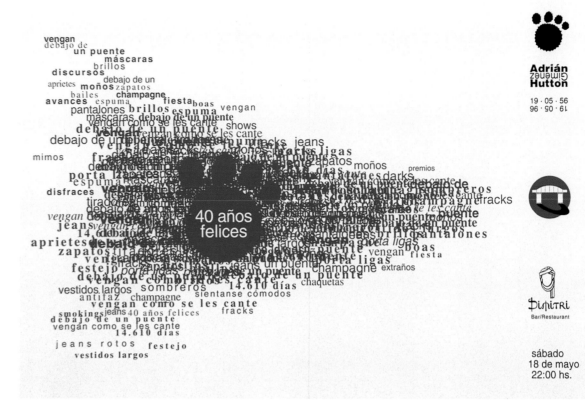

1. CD, D: Gonzalo Berro D: Macarena Ubios DF: Cato & Berro Diseño CL: Puente Mitre   Argentina 1996

2. CD, D: Gonzalo Berro D: Esteban Serrano DF: Cato & Berro Diseño CL: Puente Mitre   Argentina 1996

AD, D: Akira Utsumi P: Loe-hai, Chiong CL: Tai-gi-pan   Japan   1996

1. AD, D: Takeshi Kuroda P: Miwa Isoi DF: Office Sandscape CL: Planet Pistaccio Japan 1994

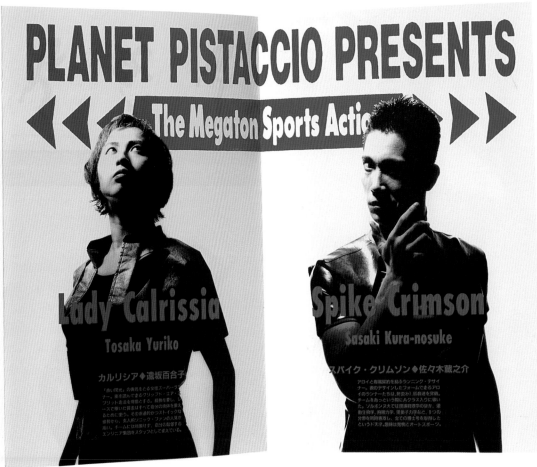

M █ 2. D: Stefanie Choi DF: NBBJ Graphic Design CL: Columbia Seafirst Center USA 1985

1. **CD, AD, D:** Leslie Chan Wing Kei **D:** Toto Tseng **DF:** Leslie Chan Design Co., Ltd. **CL:** Toppy Fashion Co., Ltd. Taiwan 1995

2. **CD:** Stuart I. Frolick **AD, D:** Darin Beaman **I:** Marla Frazee **DF, CL:** Art Center College of Design USA 1995

M ▮ 1. **CD, AD, D:** Sonia Greteman **AD, D:** James Strange **CL:** Duffens Optical   USA

2. **CD, D:** Mario A. Mirelez **DF:** Mirelez / Ross Inc. **CL:** Thomson Consumer Electronics   USA 1994   M ▮

1. **CD**: Stuart I. Frolick **AD**: Darin Beaman **D, P**: Brian Rackleff **DF, CL**: Art Center College of Design   USA   1995   M

2. **AD, D**: Shannon Beer **CL**: Shannon Beer / David Belanger   USA   1996

1. **AD, D:** Clifford Stoltze **D:** Rebecca Fagan / Peter Farrell **DF, CL:** Stoltze Design USA 1993

115

2. **CD, D:** Jane Jenkins / Tom Jenkins **CW:** Jim Thackray **DF:** The Design Foundry **CL:** The Nature Conservancy USA 1995

design industries foundation for AIDS

Tickets for the main event are $75.00. Tickets including a pre-event sit down dinner are $200.00. Reserved corporate tables for dinner seating ten people are $2000.00.

friendships to explore

and   yet so little time

pulsating
          beats
cadence   and
          rhyme
          bodies pressed together
others   held   apart
                    it
happened all so quickly
          and there you stole
my
heart

ANDY WARHOL LABEL
HEAT ■ BLOOD FOR DRACULA ■ FLESH FOR FRANKENSTEIN

1. AD, D: Jeffrey Fabian / Laura Latham / Samuel Shelton P: Geof Kern CW: Cheryl P. Duvall
DF: Kinetik Communication Graphics, Inc. CL: Design Industries Foundation for AIDS, DC USA 1991

2. CD, AD: Cinema Cats D: Masaharu Suzuki CL: Comstock Japan

LEO BURNETT IS MOVING.

1. CD, AD: Stefan Sagmeister D: Veronica Oh DF: Sagmeister Inc.   USA 1993

2. CD, AD: Stefan Sagmeister D, I: Mike Chu D: Peter Rae / Patrick Daily P: Arthur Schulten DF: The Design Group CL: Leo Burnett USA 1993

3. CD, AD: Stefan Sagmeister D, I: Susanne Poelleritzer P: Michael Grimm DF: Sagmeister Inc. CL: Fabrica USA

1. AD, D: Shannon Beer P: Craig Bailey CL: Craig Hickman   USA 1995

2. AD: Ric Riordon D: Dan Wheaton / Shirley Riordon DF: The Riordon Design Group Inc. CL: University of Toronto   Canada 1996

BELLEVUE CLUB
HOTEL

For discriminating travelers, the Bellevue Club Hotel is a very special find: a hotel only minutes from all that matters . . . and a retreat that's dramatic yet quiet. ◆ It is, for appointments and detailing, a hotel on par with the best. For feeling, it is completely its own. ◆ Artistic and original . . . imaginative and rich . . .

Here, guests enjoy the privileges of membership in unparalleled social and athletic facilities.

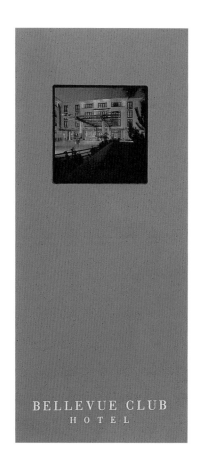

BELLEVUE CLUB
HOTEL

BELLEVUE CLUB
HOTEL

Each one of our sixty-four rooms and three suites is unique, though they share an ambience that's intimate . . . refined. ◆ At every turn, you'll find an unexpected detail . . . an original touch. ◆ From handcrafted furniture, imported fabrics, and spa bath facilities in limestone and marble . . . whether overlooking the fountain court yard, tennis, or southerly vistas to Mt. Rainier, you are surrounded by substance, grace, and strength.

CD, AD, D: Leo Raymundo P: Rocky Salskov CW: Pamela Mason Davey DF: NBBJ Graphic Design CL: Bellevue Club Hotel   USA 1995

1. CD, AD, D: J. J. F. G. Borrenbergs / R. Verkaart DF: Stoere Binken Design CL: Jean - Philippe Rieu Netherlands 1996

2. CD: Emine Tusavul AD: Yesim Kuscuoglu DF: T. T Reklam Hizmetleri CL: Foli Turkey 1996

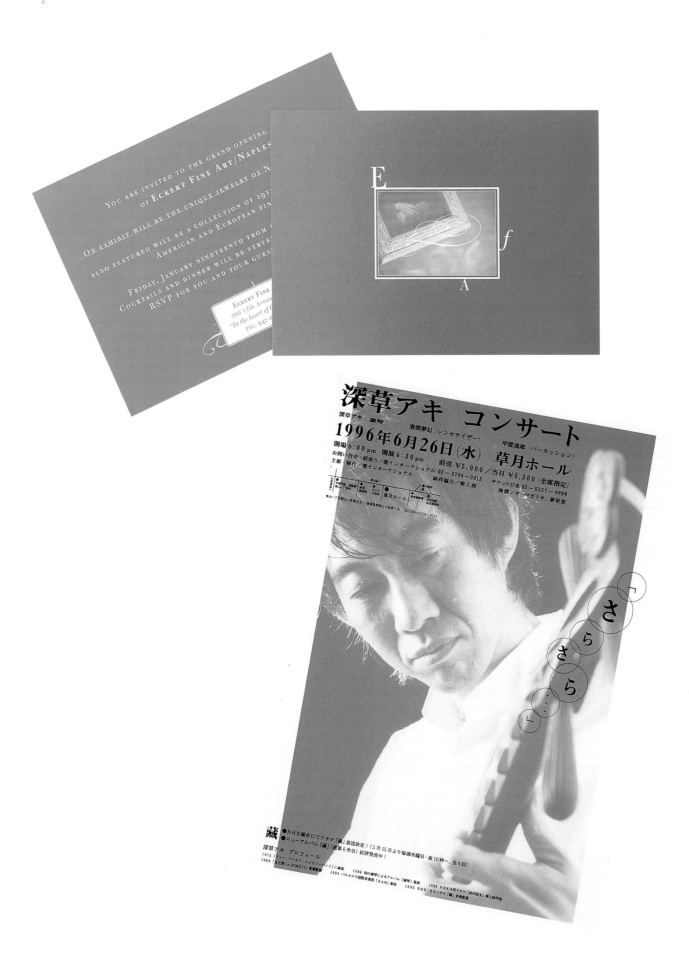

M 1. CD, AD, D: Mario A. Mirelez DF: Mirelez / Ross Inc. CL: Eckert Fine Art   USA 1995

2. AD, D: Masami Ishibashi P: Akiyoshi Miyashita DF: Masami Ishibashi Design Inc. CL: Raku International   Japan 1996

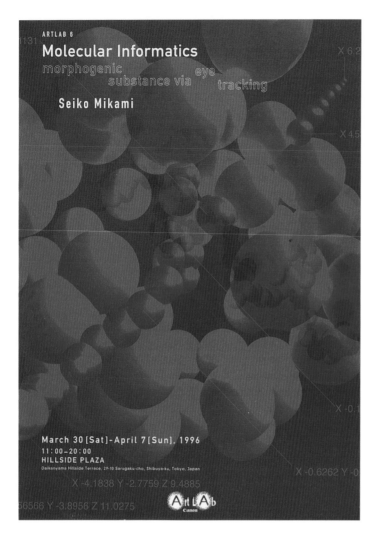

1. **AD, D:** Tomohiro Itami **Artist:** Seiko Mikami **CL:** Art Lab, Canon Inc.   Japan 1996

2. **CD:** Akihiro Suzuki **AD:** Yasunori Arai **D:** Hiroyuki Yamaguchi **P:** Tomoharu Hirata **DF:** Picture Disc **CL:** Stance Company   Japan 1992

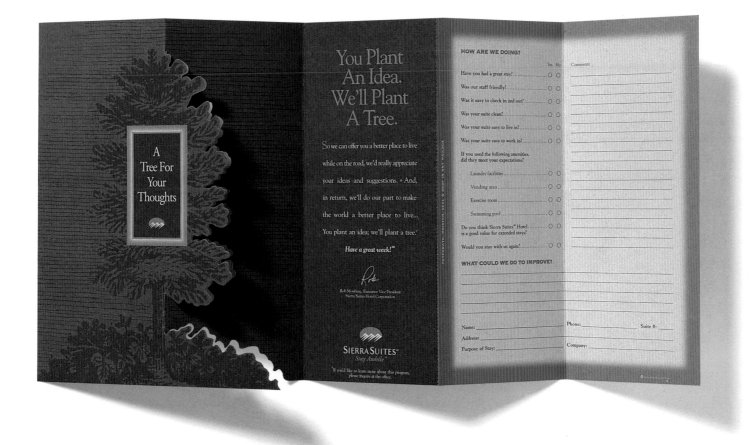

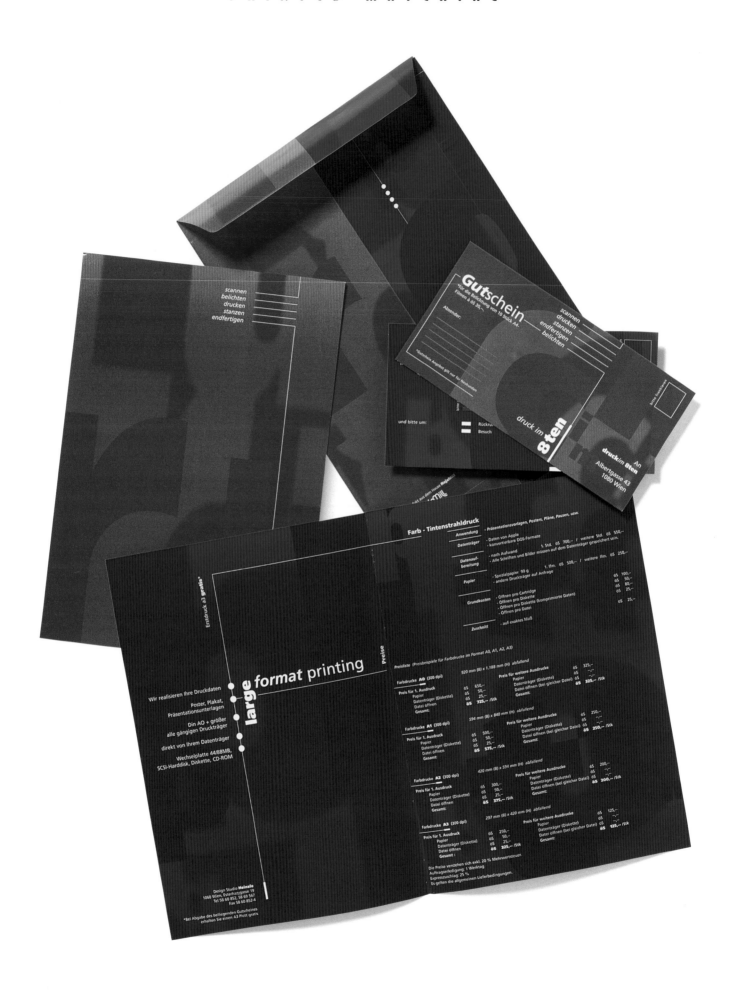

CD, AD, D, DF: Heinzle Lothar Amilian CL: Heinzle / Druck im 8ten Austria 1995

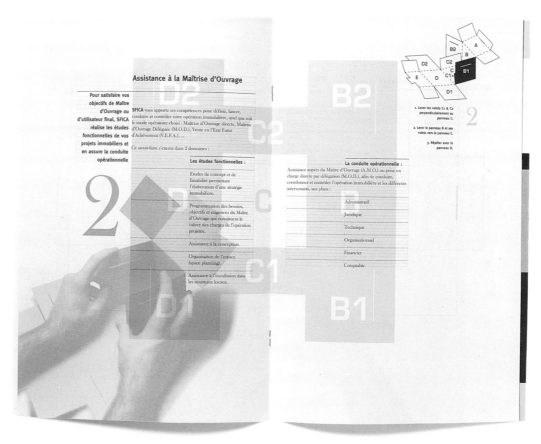

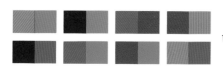

1. **AD:** Roslyn Eskind **D:** Nicola Lyon **DF:** Eskind Waddell **CL:** Avenor Inc. Canada 1996

2. **CD:** Christopher Evans **CL:** Sfica France 1994 *Cover constructs into a box

SNOW WEAR/PREMIER/'97 COLLECTION

街の雪も恋しい。
スノーウェア、プリミエ。

ゲレンデでもクールにきまるため、ストリートでは
自分らしさで清潔するために、プリミエは生まれた。
撥水性はもちろん、袖口のインナースパッツや
衿のファスナー使いなど、スノーウェアとしての
機能性もしっかりと備えながら、
コーディネイトの楽しさもファッション性も。
スノーウェアのルールをすべて新しくしてしまった。
しかも、ジャケットやベストを小さくたたむと
バッグやリュックになる可変性は、
旅のスタイルも変えてしまう。

COOL JUNCTION

COOL COLORS
ブラック、オフホワイト、シルバーというモノトーンの
クールさがプリミエの基本色。ここに'97年は
ダークレッドとクールなパステルカラーが加わりました。
おしゃれな街に映えるプリミエ。

SIMPLE
着る人のセンスを最大限に生かすためのシンプルなデザイン。
時代の要素をバランス良く取り入れたシャープなシリーズです。

LAYERED
シンプルだからできるレイヤードスタイルを、
スノーウェアに提案するプリミエ。
異なるスタイル、アイテム、素材をコーディネイトして、
冬を何通りにも着こなす楽しさを、ゲレンデと街に届けます。

COMPACT
ダウンが驚くほど小さなバッグやリュックに形を変える。
暖かさもおしゃれも手もキュートなプリミエ。

NICE PRICE
街でもゲレンデでも活躍する出番の多さを考えると、
納得の価値あるプライスです。

ほんのりキュートでクールな色とデザインは、
いつだってどこにだって着たくなる。
'97年のプリミエは、街とゲレンデと街と街、
ストリートと部屋、時代と時代、気分と気分を
クールに切り替え、つなぐ、クール ジャンクション。
街になる雪までがこんなにも
待ち遠しいそは、初めてかもしれない。

AD, D: Motoko Naruse P: Hisashi Shimizu CL: Descente, Ltd.   Japan 1996

CD: Stuart I. Frolick AD, D: Darin Beaman D: Chris Haaga P: Steven A. Heller
Writers: Jennifer Root / Geeta Sharma / Angela Rackleff DF, CL: Art Center College of Design   USA 1996

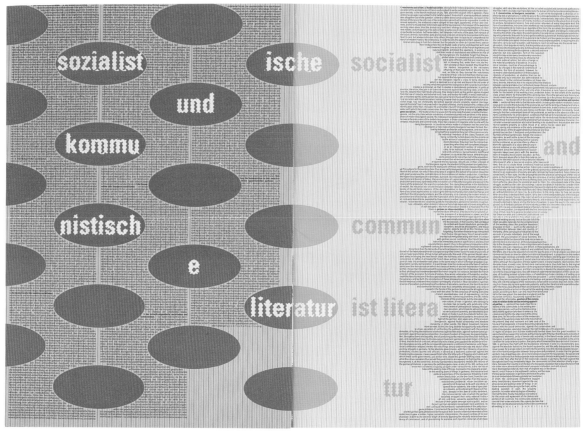

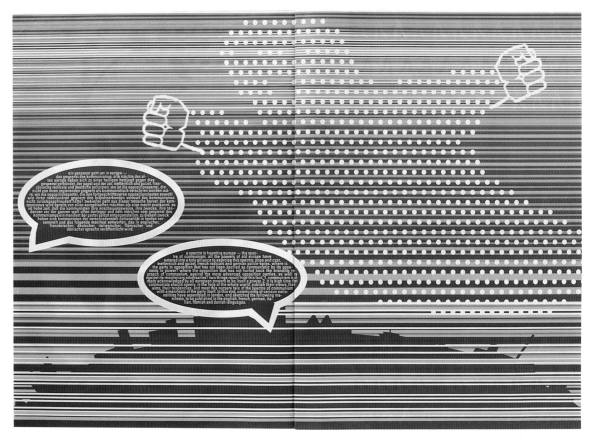

D: Detlef Fiedler D, I: Daniela Haufe DF: Cyan CL: Cyan Press Germany 1995 F F

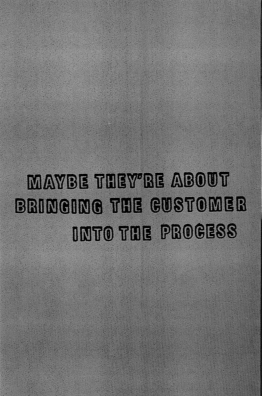

MAYBE THEY'RE ABOUT
BRINGING THE CUSTOMER
INTO THE PROCESS

MAYBE GREAT PRODUCTS
AREN'T ALWAYS PRETTY

WHERE IS YOUR NEXT
GREAT PRODUCT
GOING TO COME FROM?

CD, AD: Bill Cahan D: Bob Dinetz DF: Cahan + Associates CL: GVO, Inc. USA 1996

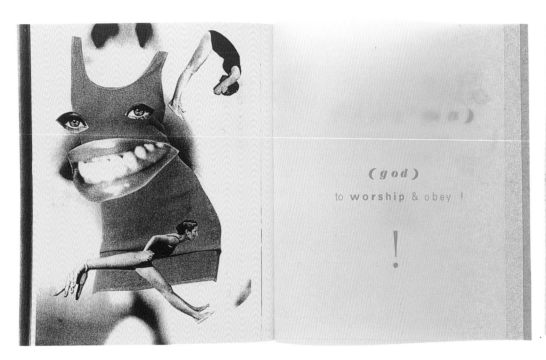

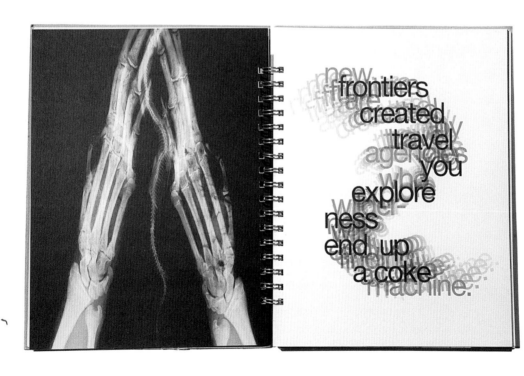

1. CD, D, P, I: Seán O'Mara DF, CL: Xon Corp UK 1993

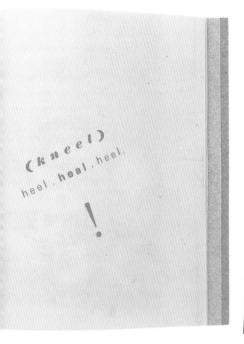

2. CD, D: Robert Bergman - Ungar AD: Giles Dunn P: Nick Knight / various DF: Bergman - Ungar Associates CL: Map Magazine USA 1996

CD: Stuart I. Frolick AD: Rebeca Mendez D: Darin Beaman DF, CL: Art Center College of Design   USA   1993

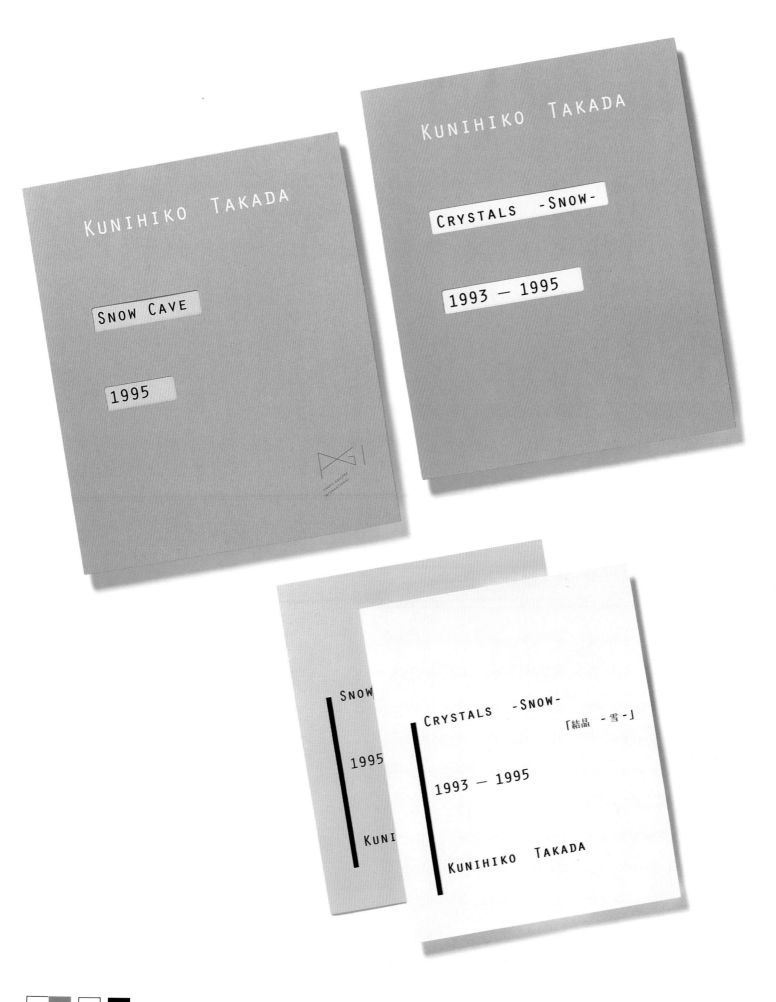

CD: Shin Yamazaki AD, D: Issay Kitagawa P: Kunihiko Takada CL: Photo Gallery International   Japan 1996

Taking **risks** requires courage and encouragement.

"It's easier because I have family, but it's also hard emotionally sometimes to do things on your own. I want to know I can do it."

See the world in a different way.

WICHITA INDUSTRIES AND SERVICES FOR THE BLIND, INC.
1995 ANNUAL REPORT

W I S B ANNUAL REPORT
WE'RE MAKIN' IT
Wichita Industries & Services For The Blind Inc.

⑧ At WISB we succeed professionally because we are encouraged to make our own choices, promoted to leadership positions, and given the authority to make key decisions. Our participation is crucial when developing policy, planning future goals, and carrying out everyday operations. Keeping the lines of communication open is a must. It isn't always easy but it is worth the effort. ✋ It wasn't too long ago that Christopher Coleman, production aide, wasn't sure he could succeed. He worked hard and soon mastered every stage of pen production. Then he started helping others any way he could. It was this initiative and demonstration of ability that promoted Christopher to production aide. At WISB, empowerment comes from within. We are the company.

"Anytime you're working for a place like this it improves your self-esteem, you feel like a first class citizen. You're making your own way rather than someone else taking care of you."

Mildred Meck, Production

E M P O W E R

WISB

1. CD, AD, D: Sonia Greteman AD, D: James Strange CL: WISB USA 1995

2. CD, AD, D: Sonia Greteman D: James Strange P: Mark Weins CL: WISB USA 1994

1. **CD**: Stuart I. Frolick **D**: Darin Beaman **DF, CL**: Art Center College of Design USA 1994

2. **CD, AD, D**: Sonia Greteman **AD, D**: James Strange / Craig Thomson **CL**: Greteman Group USA

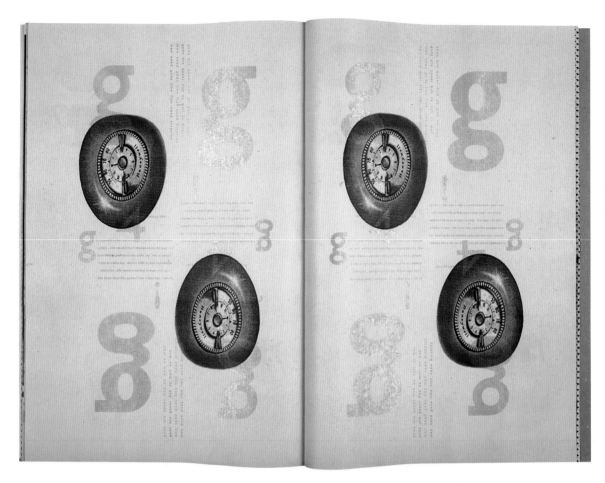

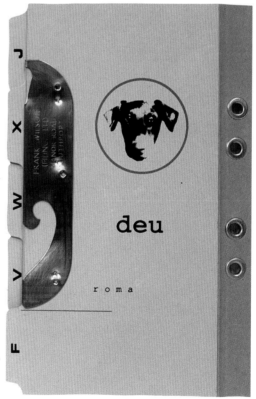

1. CD, D: Seán O'Mara DF, CL: Xon Corp   UK 1993

2. CD, D, P: Seán O'Mara DF, CL: Xon Corp   UK 1993

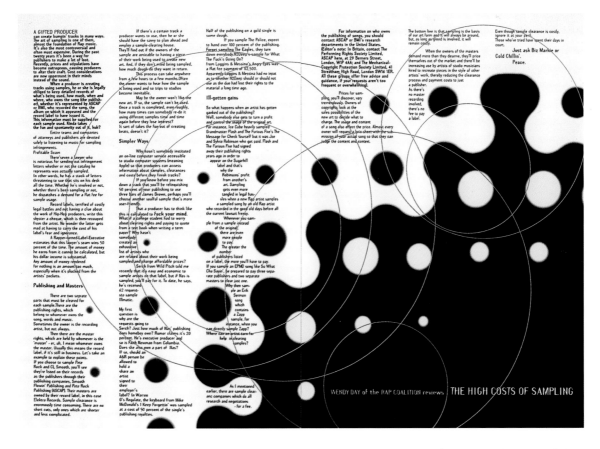

A GIFTED PRODUCER

can create bumpin' tracks in many ways. The art of sampling is one of them, almost the foundation of Rap music. It's also the most controversial and often most expensive. During the past twenty years it's been a way for publishers to make a lot of loot. Recently, prices and stipulations have become outrageous, causing producers to alter their craft. Cost considerations are now uppermost in their minds instead of the sound.

When a producer is creating tracks using samples, he or she is legally obliged to keep detailed records of what's being used, how much, when and where, who owns the song (the publisher), whether it's represented by ASCAP or BMI, who recorded the song, the album on which it appeared and the record label to trace it. This information must be supplied for each sample used. Kinda takes the fun and spontaneity out of it, huh?

Entire teams and companies of attorneys and publishers are devoted solely to listening to music for sampling infringements.

Profitable Scam

There's even a lawyer who is notorious for sending out infringement letters whether or not the catalog he represents was actually sampled. In other words, he has a stack of letters threatening to sue that sits on his desk all the time. Whether he's involved or not, whether there's been sampling or not, he dispatches a demand for a flat fee for sample usage.

Record labels, terrified of costly legal battles and not having a clue about the work of Hip-Hop producers, write this shyster a cheque, which is then recouped from the artist. No wonder the latter gets mad at having to carry the cost of his label's fear and ignorance.

A Rapper-turned-Label-Executive estimates that this lawyer's scam wins 50 percent of the time. The amount of money he earns from it cannot be calculated, but his dollar income is substantial. Any amount of money rendered for nothing is an amount too much, especially when it's plucked from the artists' pockets.

Publishing and Masters

There are two separate parts that must be cleared for each sample. There are the publishing rights, which belong to whomever owns the song, words and music. Sometimes the owner is the recording artist, but not always.

Then there are the master rights, which are held by whomever is the 'master' - er, uh, I mean whomever owns the master. Usually this means the record label, if it's still in business. Let's take an example to explain these points.

If you choose to sample Pete Rock and CL Smooth, you'll see they're listed on their records as the publishers through their publishing companies, Smooth Flowin' Publishing and Pete Rock Publishing (ASCAP). Their masters are owned by their record label, in this case Elektra Records. Sample clearance is enormously time consuming. There are no short cuts, only ones which are shorter and less complicated.

If there's a certain track a producer wants to use, then he or she should have the savvy to plan ahead and employ a sample-clearing house. They'll find out if the owners of the sample are amenable to having a piece of their work being used to create new art. And, if they don't mind being sampled, how much dough do they want in return.

This process can take anywhere from a few hours to a few months. Often the owner wants to hear how the sample is being used and so trips to studios become inevitable.

May be the owner won't like the new art. If so, the sample can't be used. Once a track is completed, even roughly, how many times can somebody re-do it using different samples time and time again before they lose interest? It sort of takes the fun out of creating beats, doesn't it?

Simpler Ways

Why hasn't somebody instituted an on-line computer service accessible to studio computer systems streaming Apple! so that producers can access information about samples, clearances and costs before they finish tracks? If you know before you mix down a track that you'll be relinquishing 50 percent of your publishing to use three Stars of James Brown, perhaps you'll choose another sample that's more user-friendly.

That a producer has to think like this is calculated to fuck your mind. What if a college student had to worry about clearing rights and paying to quote from a test book when writing a term paper? Why hasn't somebody created an exhaustive list of artists who are relaxed about their work being sampled and charge affordable prices? Serch from Wild Pitch told me recently that it's easy and economic to sample artists on that label, but if Nas is sampled, you'll pay for it. To date, he says, he's received 62 requests to sample Illmatic.

My first question is why are the requests going to Serch? Just how much of Nas' publishing does homeboy own? Rumor claims it's 20 percent. He's executive producer and so is Faith Newman from Columbia. Does she also own a part of Nas? If so, should an A&R person be allowed to hold a share an artist signed to their employer's label? Is Warren G's Regulate, the keyboard from Mike McDonald's I Keep Forgettin' was sampled at a cost of 50 percent of the single's publishing royalties.

Half of the publishing on a gold single is some dough.

If you sample The Eagles, expect to hand over 100 percent of the publishing. Forget sampling The Eagles, they turn down everybody. N2Deep's sample for What The Fuck's Going On? from Loggins & Messina's Angry Eyes was a flat fee payment of $2,500. Apparently Loggins & Messina had no input as to whether N2Deep should or should not use as the duo had lost their rights to the material a long time ago.

Ill-gotten gains

So what happens when an artist has gotten ganked out of the publishing? Well, somebody else gets to turn a profit and control the usage of the original art. For instance, Ice Cube heavily sampled Grandmaster Flash and The Furious Five's the Message for Check Yourself but it was Joe and Sylvia Robinson who got paid. Flash and The Furious Five had signed away their publishing rights years ago in order to appear on the Sugarhill label and that's why the Robinsons' profit from another's art. Sampling gets even more tangled in legal hassles when a new Rap artist samples a sampled song by an old Rap artist who recorded in the good old days before all the current lawsuit frenzy.

Whenever you sample from a sample instead of the original, there are even more people to pay. The greater the number of publishers listed on a label, the more you'll have to pay. If you sample an EPMD song like So What Cha Sayin', be prepared to pay three separate publishers and two separate masters to clear just one. Why then sample an Erik Sermon song which contains a Zapp sample, for instance, when you can directly sample Zapp? Where can an artist turn for help in clearing samples?

As I mentioned earlier, there are sample clearance companies which do all research and negotiations - for a fee.

For information on who owns the publishing of songs, you should contact ASCAP or BMI's research departments in the United States. (Editor's note: In Britain, contact The Performing Rights Society Limited, ASCAP here, at 29 Berners Street, London, W1P 4AX; and The Mechanical-Copyright Protection Society Limited, 41 Streatham High Road, London SW16 1ER. All these groups offer free advice and guidance, if your requests aren't too frequent or overwhelming.)

Prices for sampling, you'll discover, vary tremendously. Owners of copyrights look at the sales possibilities of the new art to decide what to charge. The usage and content of a song also effect the price. Almost every owner will request a lyric-sheet with the submission of your actual song so that they can judge the content and context.

The bottom line is that sampling is the basis of our art form and it will always be around, but, as long as greed is involved, it will remain costly.

When the owners of the masters demand more than they deserve, they'll price themselves out of the market and there'll be increasing use by artists of studio musicians hired to recreate pieces in the style of other artists' work, thereby reducing the clearance process and payment costs to just a publisher. As there's no master recording involved, there's no fee to pay a label.

Even though sample clearance is costly, ignore it at your peril. Those who've tried have spent their days in court.

Just ask Biz Markie or Cold Chillin'. Peace.

WENDY DAY of the RAP COALITION reviews **THE HIGH COSTS OF SAMPLING**

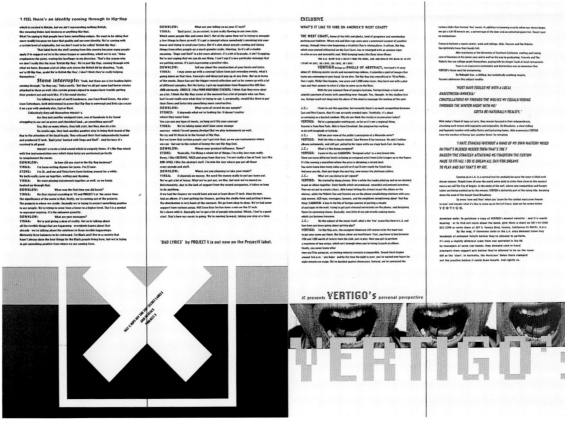

'I FEEL there's an identity coming through in Hip-Hop

EXCLUSIVE

WHAT'S IT LIKE TO VIBE ON AMERICA'S WEST COAST?

'BAD LYRICS' by PROJECT X is out now on the ProjectX label.

JC presents **VERTIGO's** personal perspective

1. **CD, AD:** Lilly Tomec / Matthias Beyrow / Marion Wagner **P:** Sebastian Lemm **CL:** HDK Berlin   Germany   1995

2. **CD, AD, D:** Lilly Tomec / Matthias Beyron / Marion Wagner **P:** Sebastian Lemm **CL:** HDK Berlin   Germany   1994

Arena Life

ウェアリー・ラブリヌスの頃は…（Japanese column text）

Arena Life is an Internet event that gathers the data of different net users under the control of a local, real-time virtual space user.

The virtual space user has her actions mapped into the Arena with a data glove and monitors this via a projection helmet; spectators monitor the Arena as a projection of the local users viewpoint. Thus, the Arena is graphically represented as a virtual 3d space for the local user and as a 2kt-Top Down Map for the exhibition audience.

The Internet user(s) enters Arena Life through their own terminal, and is defined in this space by her individual data material and knowledge/selection of other data available on the internet.

Once seen by the local user the net user(s) is invited to form data links with other net users. This appears in the virtual world as a new being. A collection of beings constitutes a 'tribe' formed from the links to the data information of each other and of the internet.

A tribe is a dynamic, growing cluster of several beings each being a databank.

Other user(s) can copy the information of the selected tribe, moving through their data, following them to their data origins.

An organic, associative data space develops.

TERRAIN, 1994

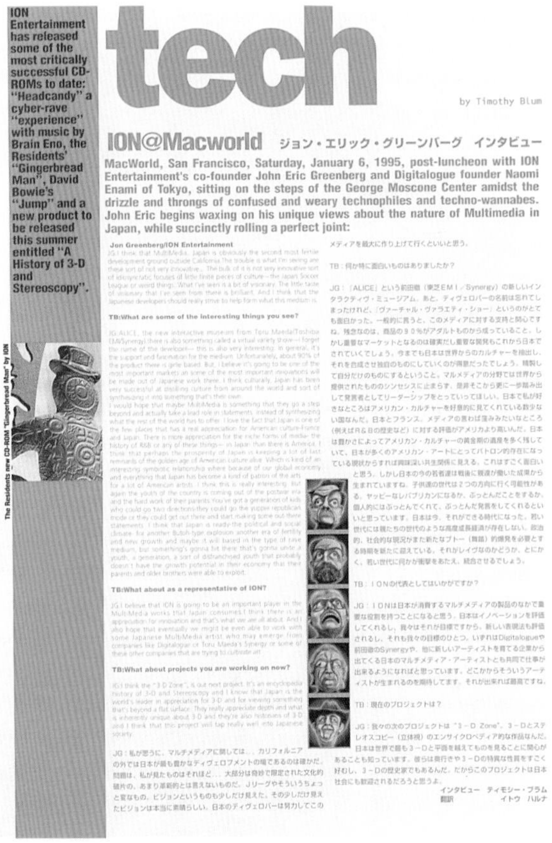

tech

by Timothy Blum

ION@Macworld

ジョン・エリック・グリーンバーグ インタヴュー

MacWorld, San Francisco, Saturday, January 6, 1995, post-luncheon with ION Entertainment's co-founder John Eric Greenberg and Digitalogue founder Naomi Enami of Tokyo, sitting on the steps of the George Moscone Center amidst the drizzle and throngs of confused and weary technophiles and techno-wannabes. John Eric begins waxing on his unique views about the nature of Multimedia in Japan, while succinctly rolling a perfect joint:

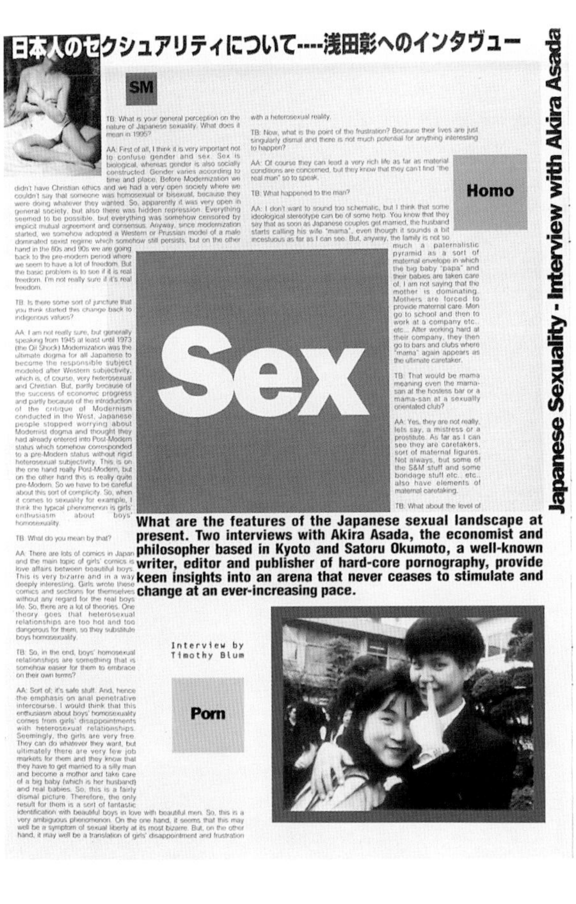

Jon Greenberg/ION Entertainment

JG: I think that Multimedia, Japan is obviously the second most fertile development ground outside California. The trouble is what I'm seeing are these sort of not very innovative... The bulk of it is not very innovative sort of wraparound, because all the fertile pieces of culture—the Japan Soccer league or weird things. What I've seen is a lot of avarice. The title side of it obvious, that I've seen here there is a brilliant, and I think that the dimension Japanese should really strive to help form what this medium is.

TB: What are some of the interesting things you see?

JG: A.I.C.L. the new interactive museum from Sony Music/Toshiba EMI/Synergy) there is also something called a virtual activity place—I forget the name of the developer—this is also very interesting. In general, it's the support and fascination for the medium. Unfortunately, about 90% of the product there is junk based. But I believe it's going to be one of the most important markets as some of the most important developers will be made out of Japanese work there. I think culturally Japan has been very successful at distilling culture from around the world and sort of synthesizing it into something that's their own.

ION Entertainment has released some of the most critically successful CD-ROMs to date: "Headcandy" a cyber-rave "experience" with music by Brain Eno, the Residents' "Gingerbread Man", David Bowie's "Jump" and a new product to be released this summer entitled "A History of 3-D and Stereoscopy".

TB: What about as a representative of ION?

JG: I believe that ION is going to be an important place in the MultiMedia works that I labor concerned. I think there is an appreciation for innovation and that's what we are all about.

TB: What about on a different level of things, on a more expressive level...

インタビュー ティモシー・ブラム
翻訳 イトウ ハルナ

日本人のセクシュアリティについて----浅田彰へのインタヴュー

Japanese Sexuality - Interview with Akira Asada

SM / Homo / Sex / Porn / Death / Panty / Daddy

What are the features of the Japanese sexual landscape at present. Two interviews with Akira Asada, the economist and philosopher based in Kyoto and Satoru Okumoto, a well-known writer, editor and publisher of hard-core pornography, provide keen insights into an arena that never ceases to stimulate and change at an ever-increasing pace.

Interview by Timothy Blum

TB: What is your general perception on the nature of Japanese sexuality. What does it mean in 1995?

AA: First of all, I think it is very important not to confuse gender and sex. Sex is biological, whereas gender is also socially constructed. Gender varies according to time and place. Before Modernization we didn't have Christian ethics and we had a very open society where we couldn't say that someone was homosexual or bisexual, because they were doing whatever they wanted. So, apparently it was very open in general society, but also there was hidden repression. Everything seemed to be possible, but everything was somehow censored by implicit mutual agreement and consensus. Anyway, since modernization started, we somehow adopted a Western or Prussian model of a male dominated sexist regime which somehow still persists, but on the other hand in the 80s and 90s we are going back to the pre-modern period where we seem to have a lot of freedom. But the basic problem is to see if it is real freedom. I'm not really sure if it's real freedom.

TB: Is there some sort of juncture that you think started this change back to indigenous values?

AA: I am not really sure, but generally speaking from 1945 at least until 1973 (the Oil Shock) Modernization was the ultimate dogma for all Japanese to become the responsible subject modeled after Western subjectivity, which is, of course, very heterosexual and Christian. But, partly because of the success of economic progress and partly because of the introduction of the critique of Modernism conducted in the West, Japanese people stopped worrying about Modernist dogma and thought they had already entered into Post-Modern status which somehow corresponded to a pre-Modern status without rigid heterosexual subjectivity. This is on the one hand really Post-Modern, but on the other hand this is maybe pre-Modern. So we have to be careful about this sort of complicity. So, when it comes to sexuality for example, I think the typical phenomenon is girls' enthusiasm about boys' homosexuality.

TB: What do you mean by that?

AA: There are lots of comics in Japan and the main topic of girls' comics is love affairs between beautiful boys. This is very bizarre and in a way deeply interesting. Girls write these comics and sections for themselves without any regard for the real boys. So, there are a lot of theories. One theory goes that heterosexual relationships are too hot and too dangerous for them, so they substitute boys homosexuality.

TB: So, in the end, boys' homosexual relationships are something that is somehow easier for them to embrace on their own terms?

AA: Sort of, it's safe stuff. And, hence the emphasis on anal penetrative intercourse. I would think that this enthusiasm about boys' homosexuality comes from girls' disappointments with heterosexual relationships. Seemingly, the girls are very free. They can do whatever they want, but ultimately there are very few job markets for them and they know that they have to get married to a silly man and become a mother and take care of is big baby (which is her husband) and real babies. So, this is a fairly dismal picture. Therefore, the only result for them in a sort of fantastic identification with beautiful boys in love with beautiful men. So, this is a very ambiguous phenomenon. On the one hand, it seems that this may well be a symptom of sexual liberty at its most bizarre. But, on the other hand, it may well be a translation of girls' disappointment and frustration

with a heterosexual reality.

TB: Now, what is the point of the frustration? Because their lives are just singularly dismal and there is not much potential for anything interesting to happen?

AA: Of course they can lead a very rich life as far as material conditions are concerned, but they know that they can't find 'the real man' so to speak.

TB: What happened to the man?

AA: I don't want to sound too schematic, but I think that some ideological stereotype can be of some help, you know. The love that they feel as soon as Japanese couples get married, the husband starts calling his wife 'mama', even though it sounds a bit incestuous as far as I can see. But, anyway, the family is not so much a paternalistic pyramid as a sort of maternal envelope in which the big baby 'papa' and their babies are taken care of. I am not saying that the mother is dominating. Mothers are forced to provide maternal care. Men go to bars and clubs where 'mama' again appears as the ultimate caretaker.

TB: That would be mama meaning over the mama-san at the hostess bar or a mama-san at a sexually orientated club?

AA: Yes, they are not really, let's say, a mistress or a prostitute. As far as I can see because they are caretakers, sort of maternal figures. Not always, but some of the S&M stuff and some bondage stuff etc., etc., also have elements of maternal caretaking.

TB: What about the level of photographer. So, this is a sort of heterosexual mechanism of recuperating the straightforward images. But on the other hand, there are other photographers and other artists who are really making quite straightforward expressions and in those cases they have to face censorship.

TB: From my perspective there is a very strong thought that 'My God, it's really unbelievable that we're in 1995 and in Japan' - it's a very simple story, but - 'you can't show this or this or this and that leads to some other thing that is just not what I expected and which may lead to some strange action' -violence? - I don't know if this has to do with S&M or bondage or things like that. What do you think about this?

AA: Well, generally speaking I think that censorship and the particular legislation about sexual expression is simply outmoded and I don't think they are really pertinent to the present situation. But what bothers me is a sort of implicit censorship when it comes to literature or art etc., and also this implicit mechanism of recuperating the really dangerous images and literary stuff into an understandable, human context - that's one thing. The other thing is that real censorship is not only about the expression of sexual activities, but always about the implicit relationship between sex and politics. Now I am thinking about Oe Kenzaburo's...

TB: Can you explain this case?

AA: Recently Oe was awarded the Nobel Prize. The story goes that it started in '63 when his child was born with a huge handicap and he went to Horseman and ended up with the literary salvation of personal tragedy through thirty years of literary work. Ok that's fine. But, something happened before '63. In 1960, the chairman of the Socialist Party was assassinated by a 17 year old boy of the Right Wing. So, Oe was shocked and immediately after the assassination, he wrote a sort of diptych - '17' and 'A Political Boy Dies'. '17' was published in the January issue of 'Bungalo Kai'- the latter part in the February issue. It was a sort of psychological or almost psycho-analytical description of a young onanist who is too self-conscious to be on his own, but who ultimately identifies with the Right Wing and for whom the fantasy of identification with the emperor and his army is the ultimate key to orgasm. So it's about male fantasy, which is the basis of some right wing fascist movements. So, of course the Right Wing was enraged and actually at the same time Fukazawa Shichiro wrote a grotesque parody- this was a grotesque novel called 'Furyu Mutan' in which in some sense describes the decapitation of the crown prince and his wife. So both these works became scandalous and the Right Wing threatened Oe and his publisher as well as Fukazawa and his publisher and went as far as to kill

frustration on the part of the man with the wife/mother sexually speaking. Is there some sexual dissatisfaction with the wife/mother and therefore they are using some sort of surrogate figure? For example, I mean you're frustrated with your wife/mother and when you've finished work, you go out, get sucked and...

AA: go to clubs and sex clubs. But, again ultimately they are seeking a sort of caretaker for their sexual frustrations, so in that sense they are simply seeking a second mother or whatever. Maybe I'm talking too much.

TB: But, do both parties have responsibility for this? Is it societies' responsibility or are these two both frustrated with each other or what?

AA: Ultimately, so far as this society is male-chauvinistic, I think this is the man's responsibility. But, I don't think that men can liberate both themselves and women. I think that the best solution is brought about by women. I hope that Japanese women will simply leave the family, leave their children so that children can be liberated from excessive maternal protection to go out on their own, while mothers have something to do as professionals and I don't expect Japanese men to be really independent. I would rather hope that Japanese women have more political and public activities, so that they can leave their children quite young, so that they can leave their children.

TB: So the real change will be within the next generation - not the father/baby, but the young children that will be influenced by this departure.

AA: I think so. This phenomenon was already starting as far as I can see in the 70s and 80s. Growth became solitary and can find their own ways. So I am not really too pessimistic about it, but am also totally pessimistic about this situation.

TB: What about on a different level of things, on a more expressive level. For example, perhaps Nobuyoshi Araki, his function and his relationship to censorship and maybe censorship's relationship to repression, if you had any relationship. I don't know. What do you think about this issue, which has I guess over the last year really come to the foreground?

AA: Yes. Well, I'm not really sure because in Araki's case, even though his pictures are very straightforward, on the other hand Araki provides some personal context in which these pictures are somehow recuperated. In literature we have a tradition of the 'I' novel where the author speaks of his own life - the death of his wife, the desperate life etc., So Araki is in a way strictly following this model of the 'I' novel - the death of his own wife etc., etc., So, even though his pictures sometimes look very straightforward and violent, the audience can understand them as parts of the 'I' novel - the anarchic, but sympathetic life of the solitary

Fukazawa's publisher's maid. So it was a big scandal. It was in '61. So , anyway it was a big trauma for Oe about him in '63 he had this personal tragedy, he went to Hiroshima and the rest of the story is well known. But , I think the second part of '17' - 'A Political Boy Dies' - is still censored - not legality of course, but no publisher is willing to publish it even though he is now a Nobel Laureate. So, it's this sort of implicit relation between sexuality and politics which is really hot stuff for the Right Wing and for publishers. So, I do think that this kind of implicit censorship is still working.

TB: Do the Right Wing actually have a lot of influence? Are they actually influencing - on a very basic level again - visual censorship, in terms of the visual arts?

AA: No, this is another story. I think it is rather parents or simply conservative people. The Right Wing has some sexual complexes of their own, so they are sensitive towards the works of Mishima and Oe and others.

TB: But again, there is the perception that if you cover or hide certain things then obviously there are certain psychological repercussions. If you constantly cannot directly see what's going on in a situation (whether its political or actually just sexual) do you think that this perception is true? Do you think that there are any uncanny Japanese situations that arise because of this?

AA: To a certain extent yes. Actually, Japanese pornography is much more pornographic because they cannot show the parts. So they can become really obscene without showing the parts. And of course it gives rise to the various types of underground sexual activities, such as SM and bondage etc. Again, I don't have this perception that censorship is really the actual problem. This is a remnant of the past. They have no reason to do it today.

TB: Do you think censorship will ever be dropped?

AA: Well, it's possible, but I'm not really sure because Japanese politics is in a stalemate so no one really can change the situation.

TB: What do you think it would be like, for example, if you were not you, but were a Japanese person sexually 'coming of age' these days. What do you think it would be like? What kinds of things are they going to confront? How would it be unique, other than if you were growing up in Alabama or a suburb of Paris? Do you think there is any unique situation or unique conditions?

AA: Well, I'm not really sure that the Japanese situation is really unique. But, no doubt they are faced with a sort of dual situation. On the imaginary level - I mean on the level of mass media imagery or publications or video etc., - there are a lot of freedoms, everything is possible. It is a sort of paradise. But on the real level it is the old dismal situation. And also the same thing applies here, because the girls can fantasize in a very colorful way about they're sexual activities or some boys' homosexuality etc. But, as far as I can see, it is a compensation of harsh reality. On the other hand, what boys are doing is to keep up with girls expectations. So, I think that Japanese boys are really, really prissy nowadays. Maybe they are the prettiest in the world. But, it doesn't mean that they are sexy. They are simply pretty. They are simply beautiful dolls dancing on Television. They are really beautiful, it's phenomenal. But, he has to act according to the girls expectation and the girls' obscene without showing the parts And of course it gives rise to the various types of nightmarish situation, even though it is a very colorful expression. So, girls are disappointed with their possible future; therefore, the last resort for them is the colorful fantasy and boys can't keep up with girls' fantasies, but that's the only way to catch girls.

TB: What about the schoolgirl thing? Not only amongst themselves, but also the uses of the schoolgirl image, or the embracing of the school girl image, or even schoolgirls (for all I know) by the heavy fantasies of Japanese society. They can be constantly in the magazines- snotgirls, schoolgirl uniforms, even the 'Buru-sera' (the panty shops, swimsuit shops, sweatsuit shops). What about this?

AA: I think this is very strange. And, of course, admittedly, it is the society who is responsible for the situation. But on the surface, I think the girls are playing the games for money or for fun. Even though adults are exploiting girls, they are sort of miserable buyers who have no other opportunity to satisfy themselves; I think it is a very complex situation. I don't think girls are victims of adults. Girls are actively playing the games, but again this is because of some frustration, deep frustration on their part. But, anyway, the fathers and the adults are seemingly repressed before 63, but despite them, but they pretend to be nice to them only for money or fun. And it's not about prostitution, its not about the real physical exploitation, so they needn't be afraid of real physical harm. Maybe it's a nice mechanism. I'm not sure. The girls are actively playing the game, even if it is the compensation of real frustration. And, I really don't know what boys are thinking about. They are simply using a lot of resources and time to become pretty to be attractive to girls.

Pink Films run at an average length of about 60 minutes, are shot in four to five days and are produced at the surprisingly low budget of exactly ¥3,500,000.Most have no artistic content; including a few sex scenes suffices to make these films commercially viable, and allows filmmakers the freedom to produce almost whatever they want. For this reason, a few outstanding films are occasionally found among them; the pornography being merely a vehicle to raise the budget for their films. Gay movies too, have derived from the world of pink cinema. These films recently provoked strong reactions abroad and many of them are banned in Europe. At the San Francisco Gay & Lesbian Film Festival '94, where many Gay Pink Films were presented, most of the audience left the theater because of the films explicit graphic content. The Japanese audience are more easy going, in the words of one director: "[The Japanese audience] usually don't have tengo to Gay Film Theaters to watch these films."

CD: Barbara Cuniberti **AD, D:** Carolyn O'Connell **DF, CL:** Kuni Graphic Design Company   Italy   1996

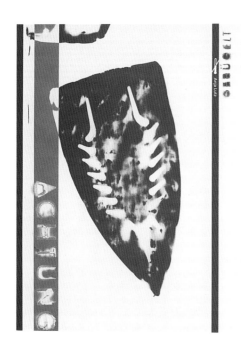

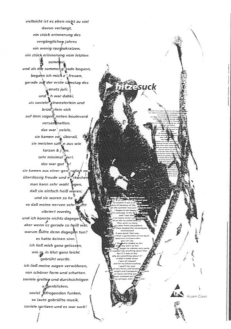

CD, AD: Lilly Tomec / Anja Lutz   CL: Shift   Germany   1996

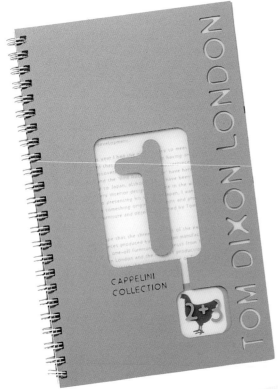

TOM DIXON

I first heard Tom Dixon's name seven years ago in London. I was in a gallery and his 'Bull Chair' was being exhibited. It had a unique design and used a frying pan positioned upside down as the seat; this is something that uniquely belongs to the world of Tom Dixon. I experienced an instant affinity for Dixon's work, purchased the 'Bull', and ever since kept an eye on his development.

Earlier this year I had the opportunity to meet him in London and learned that he was interested in having an exhibition in Japan. I discovered that his recent masterpieces, including the 'S' Chair and the 'Bird Rocking Chair' have hardly been introduced to Japan, although both have been featured in almost every interior design magazine in the world. In addition to presenting his work to Japan, I wanted the E&Y Co to achieve something original – to edit and produce a special range of furniture and objects designed by Tom with Tokyo in mind.

It is my hope that the three elements of the exhibition – masterpieces produced by the Italian manufacturer Cappellini, one-off furniture and objects from Tom's SPACE workshop in London and the new E&Y production range. – will demonstrate the extensive range of Tom's talent and creative energy.

Yoichi Nakamuta
E&Y Co

THE STORY SO FAR

Born in 1959 in Tunisia, Tom Dixon lived in Morocco and Egypt before moving to Huddersfield in Yorkshire. Moving to London aged 6, Dixon started his first creative experiments with flames, setting fire to his bedroom, much to his parents dismay.

The experiments continued eighteen years later, when mesmerised by the sparks created by the welding torch in a friends garage, he begged a lesson. At the time a promotor in the nightclub and warehouse party business, days were left free to scavenge scrapyards for the raw materials. Industrial rubbish and victorian cast-offs suggested furniture forms to Dixon's deranged mind.

The first few peculiar structures sold easily creating space and finance for a new collection and a ten year burst of feverish creative activity followed during which the work has been exhibited throughout the world, bought by princesses, pop stars, hairdressers and museums.

About 800 chairs later Tom Dixon needs to slow down and give some other people a break, thus he opens a new central London shop, SPACE an experimental outlet for new talents.

TO BE CONTINUED

CD, AD, D: Fabian Monheim CD, AD, D, I, **Type Face:** Sophia Wood P: Dan Burn Forti **DF:** Fly **CL:** E&Y 1994

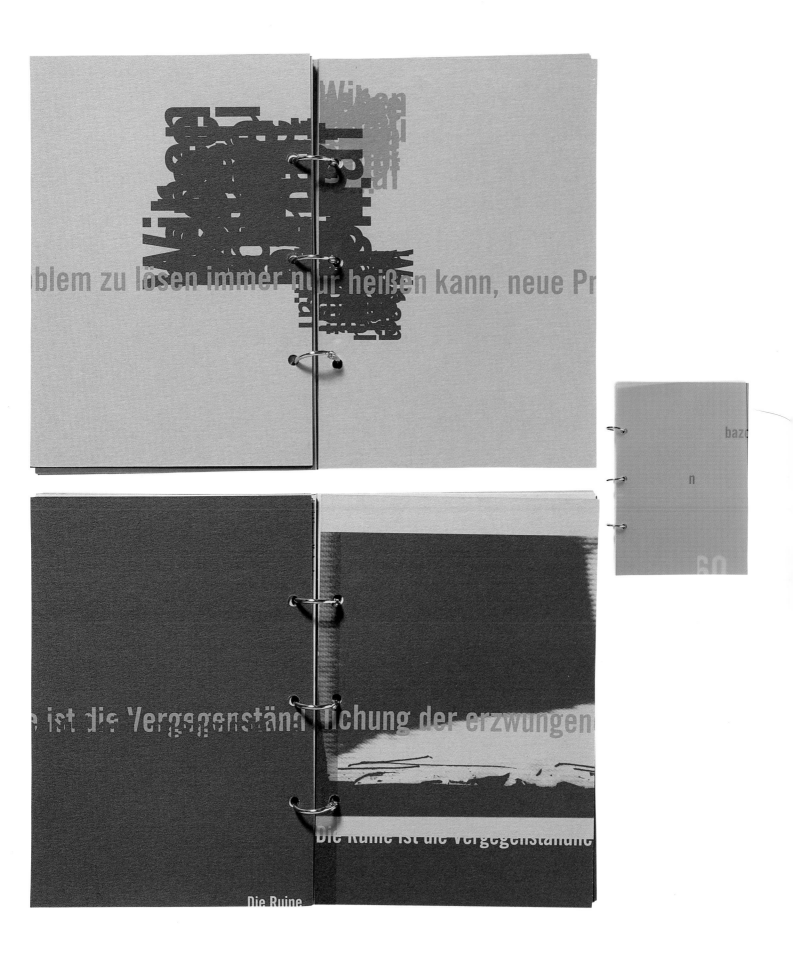

AD: Christian Boros D: Ingo Maak / Frank Müller CL: Boros Agentur Fuer Kommunikation Germany 1996

D, I: Daniel R. Smith Author: Roderick Romero DF: Command Z USA 1995

CD, AD: Koji Mizutani   D: Masashi Yamashita   P: Hibiki Kobayashi   DF, CL: Mizutani Studio   Japan   1993

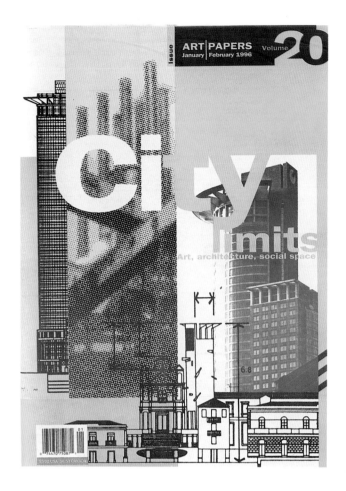

ART | PAPERS
January | February 1996
Volume
Issue

20

ci ty
limits
Art, architecture, social space

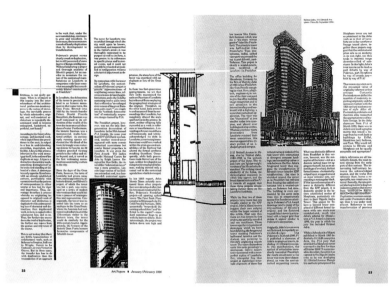

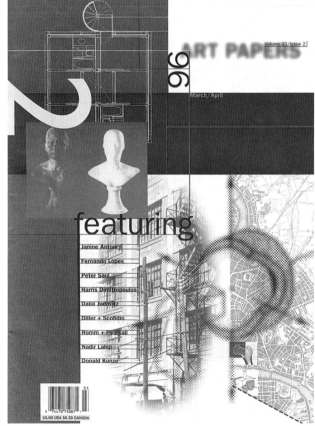

ART PAPERS
Volume 20/Issue 2
96
March/April

featuring

Janine Antoni

Fernando Lopes

Peter Saul

Harris Dimitropoulos

Dalia Judovitz

Diller + Scofidio

Romm + Pearsall

Nadir Lahiji

Donald Kunze

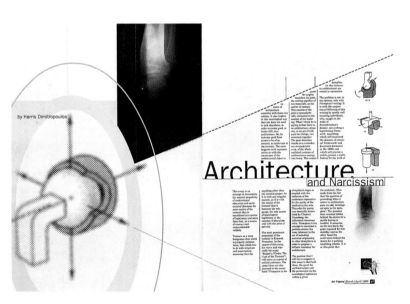

by Harris Dimitropoulos

Architecture
and Narcissism

CD, D: Pattie Belle Hastings AD, D: Bjorn Akselsen D: Brock Holt / Linda Armstrong DF: Icehouse Design CL: Art Papers Magazine USA 1996

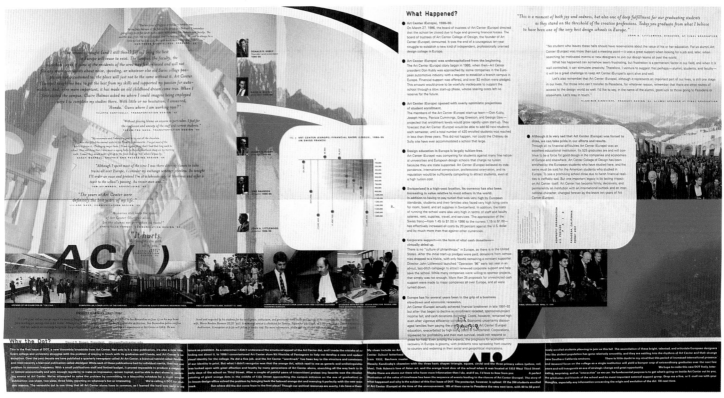

CD: Stuart I. Frolick   AD, D: Darin Beaman   D: John Choe   P: Steven A. Heller   DF, CL: Art Center College of Design   USA   1996

Print it Black
Taku Tashiro

TOM'S BOX

1. AD, D, I: Taku Tashiro DF: Taku Tashiro Office CL: Tom's Box Japan 1993

2. AD, D: Katsumi Komagata CL: One Stroke Co., Ltd. Japan 1995

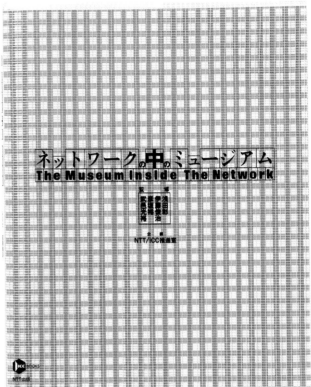

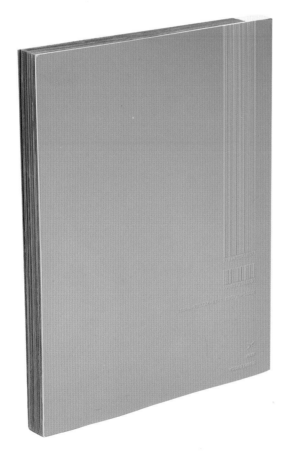

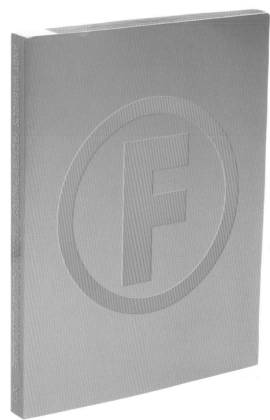

1. AD: Gento Matsumoto D: Aoi Nishiuchi / Kei Kasai CL: NTT Publishing Co., Ltd. Japan 1995

2. CD: Takashi Asai AD, D: Tomohiro Itami D: Yukio Abe CL: Uplink Japan 1996

M F

1. CD: Curt Schreiber AD: Melissa Waters D: Ken Fox P: Midcoast Studio DF: VSA Partners, Inc. CL: Harley - Davidson Motor Co.   USA 1996

2. CD, AD: Curt Schreiber AD, D: Adam Smith D: Jeff Breazeale P: James Schnepf / Ken Fox DF: VSA Partners, Inc. CL: Robert Vogele USA 1995

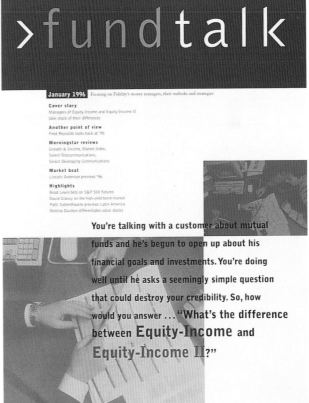

 1. AD, D: Clifford Stoltze D: Kyong Choe / Heather Kramer / Joe Polevy P: Craig MacCormack DF: Stoltze Design CL: Fidelity Investments USA 1995

2. AD: Clifford Stoltze D: Dina Radeka / Eric Norman / Heather Kramer / Wing Ip Ngan / Tracy Schroder / Brett Snyder DF: Stoltze Design
CL: Fidelity Investments USA 1996

「亜細亜散歩」
Promenade in Asia

CD: Tetsuo Fukaya AD, D: Motoko Naruse P: Taishi Hirokawa CL: Shiseido Co., Ltd.   Japan 1994

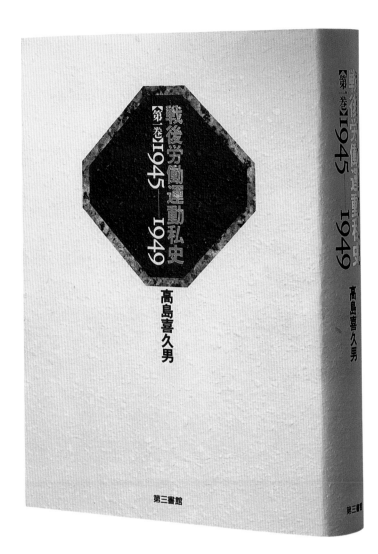

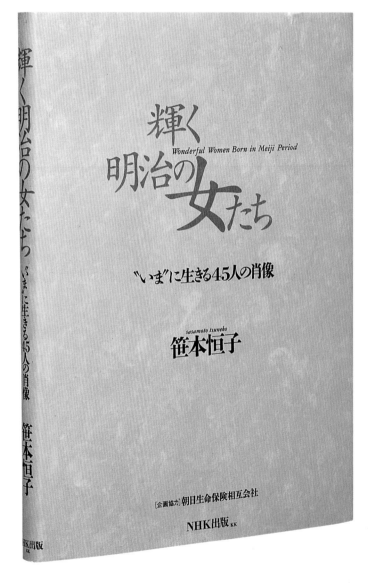

1. AD, D: Koji Ise CL: Daisanshokan Japan 1992

2. AD, D: Koji Ise CL: NHK Shuppan Japan 1992

D: Akihiko Tsukamoto CL: Yamashita Japanese Language School   Japan   1996

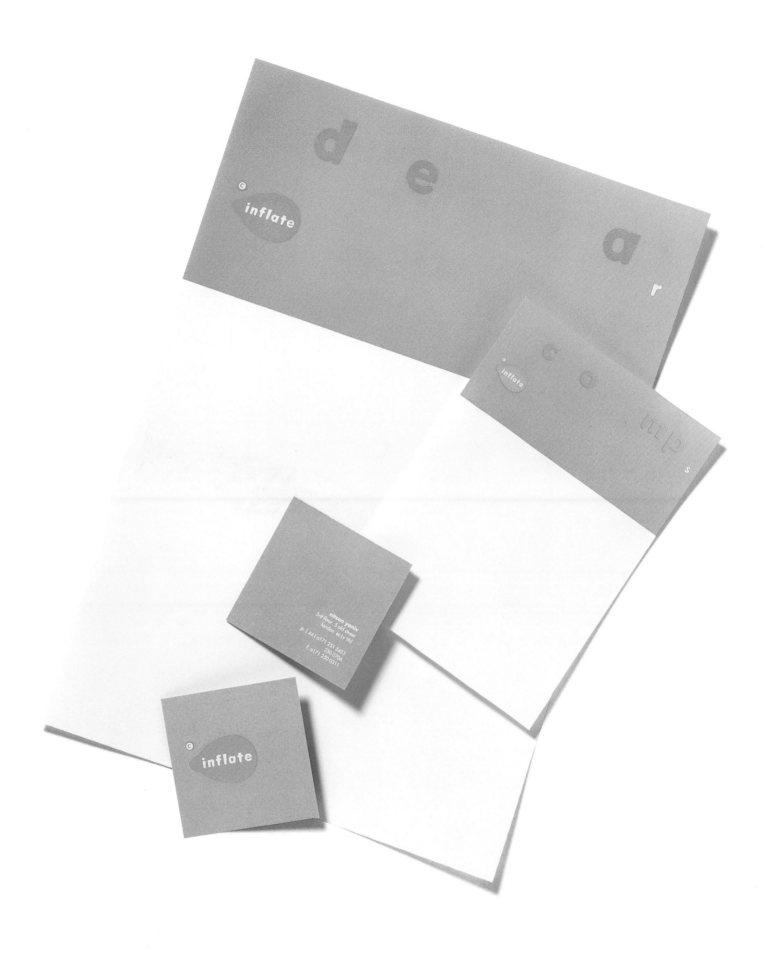

F   D: Simon Clark P: Jason Tozer CL: Inflate   UK

1, 2, 3. **CD**: 2. Yasuko Yoshida / Sayaka Yamaguchi 3. Hiromix **AD, D, I**: Gugi Akiyama
CL: 1. Gugi Akiyama 2. Sayaka Yamaguchi 3. Hiromix   Japan 1995

4. **CD, AD, D, P**: Rachel Miles **DF, CL**: Rachel Miles Design   Australia 1995

5. **CD, AD, D**: J. J. F. G. Borrenbergs / R. Verkaart **DF**: Stoere Binken Design **CL**: Yosh / Nash Design   Netherlands 1996

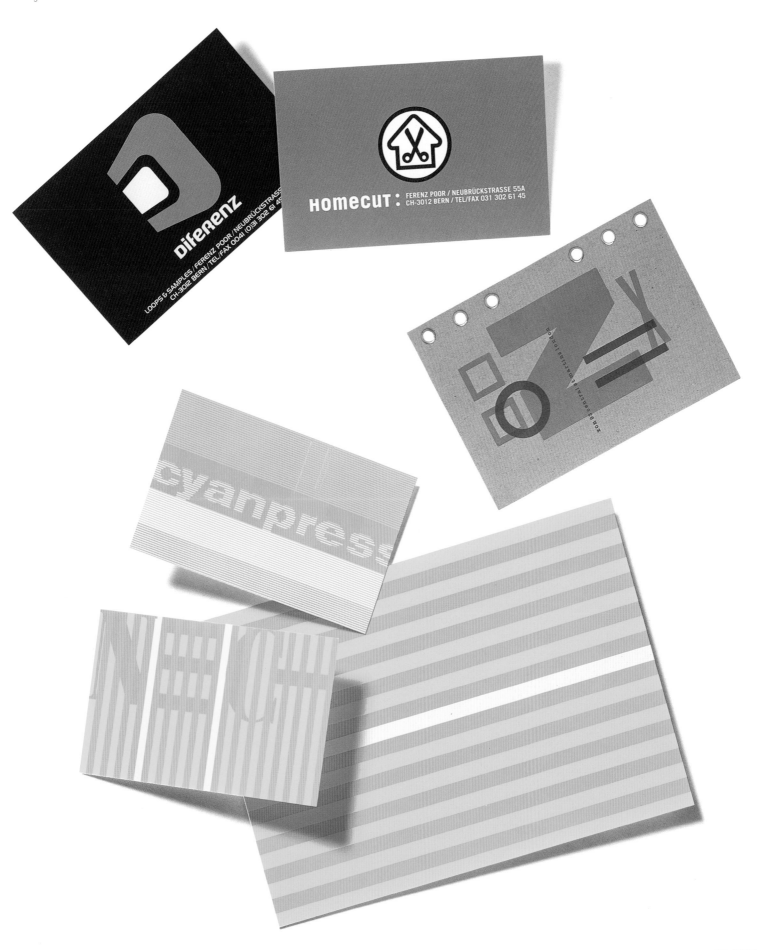

1. **AD, D:** Marc Bastard Brunner **DF:** Büro Destruct **CL:** Diferenz   Switzerland   1996

M 2. **CD, D:** Seán O'Mara **DF, CL:** Xon Corp   UK   1993

3. **D:** Daniela Haufe **DF, CL:** Cyan   Germany   1996

AD, D: Yukio Ikoma P: Yasuto Okumura CL: I'm Co., Ltd. Japan 1996

1
—
2

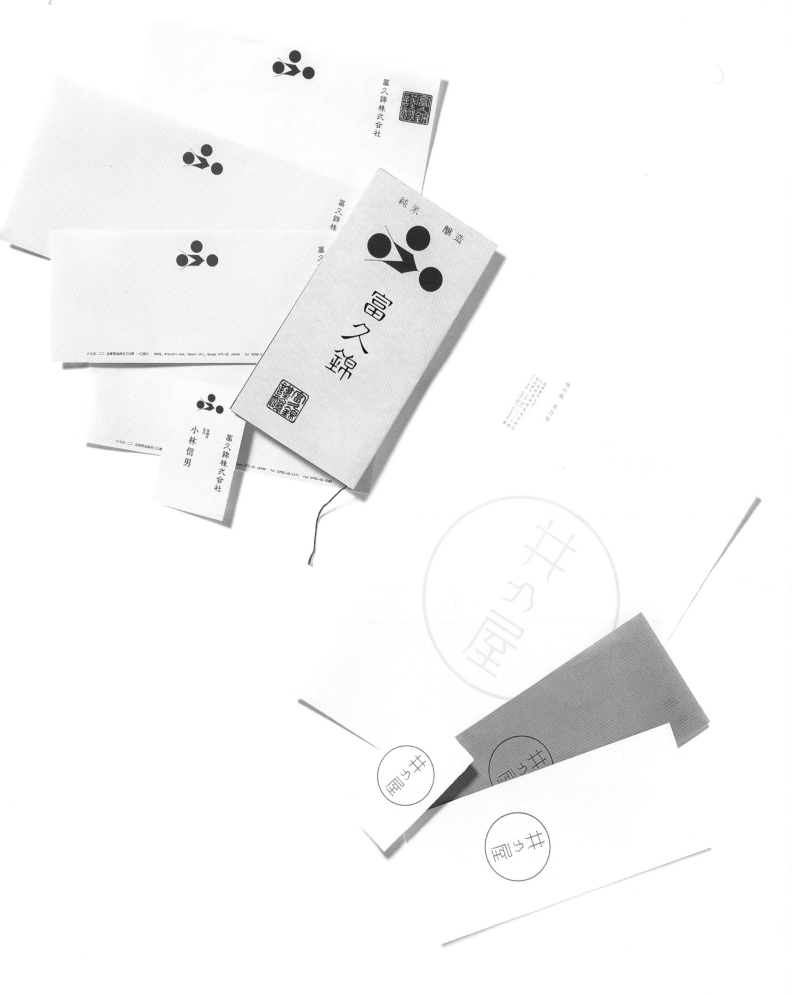

1. **CD, AD, D:** Issay Kitagawa **CL:** Fukunishiki Co., Ltd.   Japan 1995

2. **CD, AD, D:** Issay Kitagawa **CL:** Ajinokura Inoya   Japan 1996

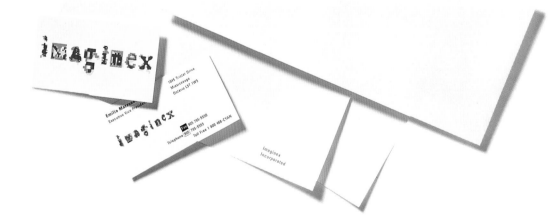

1. **CD, AD, D:** J. J. F. G. Borrenbergs / R. Verkaart **DF:** Stoere Binken Design **CL:** Eevo Lute Muzique   Netherlands 1995   M

2. **CD, AD, D:** Malcolm Waddell **D:** Maggi Cash / Nicola Lyon / Florence Ngan / Gary Mansbridge
DF: Eskind Waddell **CL:** Imaginex Inc.   Canada 1995

1. **AD**: Rick Lambert **D**: Ben Phillips **DF**: Rick Lambert Design Consultants **CL**: Dromaius Australia   Australia   1994

161

2. **CD, AD, D**: Sonia Greteman **D**: James Strange / Karen Hogan **CL**: Kansas Health Foundation   USA
*Varnish

AD: Kris Rodammer D: Keiko Hayashi **Printer:** Julie Holcomb Printers **DF, CL:** Corey McPherson Nash USA

1. **D**: Sandy Gin **DF, CL**: Sandy Gin Deisgn USA 1995

F 2. **DF**: Myriad Inc. **CL**: Rebecca Hansen Carrer USA 1996

CD, AD, D: J. J. F. G. Borrenbergs / R. Verkaart DF, CL: Stoere Binken Design Netherlands 1995
*Varnish

1. **AD, D:** Andrew Hoyne **I:** Angela Ho / Simone Elderi **DF:** Andrew Hoyne Design **CL:** Geo   Australia

2. **AD, D, I:** Andrew Hoyne **DF:** Andrew Hoyne Design **CL:** Pace Event Management   Australia   1995

1. CD, AD, D, P: Issay Kitagawa CL: Kasai City   Japan 1996

2. CD: Yasuhiko Sakura CD, AD, D: Katsunori Aoki I: Ichiro Tanida / Seijiro Kubo DF: Sun-Ad Co., Ltd. CL: Laforet Harajuku Co., Ltd.   Japan 1996

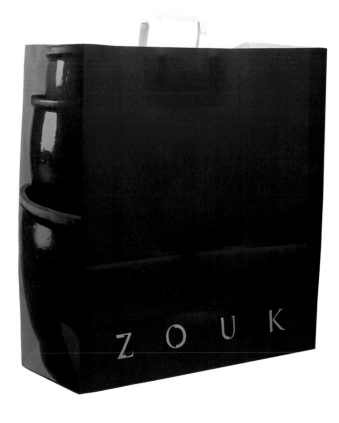

1. **CD**: Stephen Kavanagh **AD, D**: Amanda Brady **P**: Ruth Hurley **DF**: Design Factory **CL**: Hammet Ltd.   Ireland   1996

2. **CD**: Alan Chan **AD**: Miu Choy **DF**: Alan Chan Design Company **CL**: Il Colpo / Architech Studio   Hong Kong   1995

1. **AD, D, I**(L): Motoko Naruse **D**: Kyoka Tsuchiya **I**(R): Katsu Yoshida **CL**: Issey Miyake Inc. Japan 1995

2. **AD**: Katsunori Hironaka **DF**: Hironaka Design Office **CL**: Joaquin Berao Japan Japan 1996

3. **AD, D**: Katsumi Komagata **DF**: One Stroke Co., Ltd. **CL**: F. D. C. Products Inc. Japan 1996 M

AD, D: Katsu Kimura **P:** Yutaka Okada **I:** Chizuru Nakajima **DF:** Katsu Kimura & Packaging Direction Co., Ltd. **CL:** Zonart & Co., Ltd. Japan 1996

1. CD: Sonia Greteman / Paul Hanson AD, D: James Strange   USA

2. CD, AD: Sonia Greteman D: James Strange   USA

1. **AD, D:** Taku Sato **DF:** Taku Satoh Design Office Inc. **CL:** Takara Shuzo Co., Ltd. Japan 1993

2. **AD, D:** Taku Sato **DF:** Taku Satoh Design Office Inc. **CL:** The Calpis Food Industry Co., Ltd. Japan 1993

1. AD, D: Tadanori Itakura CL: Phil International Inc.   Japan

2. AD, D: Taku Sato PD: Unison Network DF: Taku Satoh Design Office Inc. CL: Takara Shuzo Co., Ltd.   Japan   1992

M   1. **CD, AD, D:** Leslie Chan Wing Kei **DF:** Leslie Chan Design Co., Ltd. **CL:** Shanghai Elan Cosmetics Co. Taiwan 1993

175

2. **CD, AD, D:** Leslie Chan Wing Kei **DF:** Leslie Chan Design Co., Ltd. **CL:** Nu Skin Taiwan Inc. Taiwan 1995   M

1. **AD, D:** Gento Matsumoto **D:** Gabin Ito **CL:** Sanyo Shokai Ltd.   Japan   1995

2. **AD:** Gento Matsumoto **D:** Kei Kasai **CL:** Sanyo Shokai Ltd.   Japan   1995   M

3. **AD, D:** Gento Matsumoto **CL:** Sanyo Shokai Ltd.   Japan   1995

1. AD: Yoshiro Kajitani D: Mayumi Kawabe DF: Kajitany Design CL: Victor Entertainment, Inc. Japan 1995

2. AD, D, I: Yoshiro Kajitani DF: Kajitany Design CL: Polydor K. K. Japan 1991

1. CD, **AD**: Stefan Sagmeister **D**: Veronica Oh **P**: Tom Schierlitz **DF**: Sagmeister Inc. **CL**: Razor & Tie   USA

2. CD, **AD, I**: Stefan Sagmeister **D**: Veronica Oh **DF**: Sagmeister Inc. **CL**: Studio SGP   USA   1995

Thank you for this purchase.

We have truly made every effort to keep the price of our fonts to a minimum so as many as possible can enjoy the beauty of typographic explorations. PLEASE DO NOT COPY THE FONT ILLEGALLY. We extend liberties to you beyond the law (each fonts comes with a 10 printer license, additional fonts are half price for the same location, and just to output your works, doesn't have to buy a copy your service bureau doesn't have to buy a copy your service bureau doesn't have to buy a copy return that you comply with our request so we may bring you more varieties in the future.

[T-26]

CD, AD, D, I: Carlos Segura I: Tony Klassen / Hatch / Tim Marcus DF: Segura Inc. CL: [T-26] USA 1996

1. AD, D: Yasuhiro Sawada CL: Nippon Columbia Co., Ltd. Japan 1993

2. CD, AD, D: Carlos Segura P: Bettman Archives DF: Segura Inc. CL: Q101 USA 1995

1996

1996

AD, D, I: Taku Tashiro D: Masato Araki DF: Taku Tashiro Office CL: The Table Japan 1995

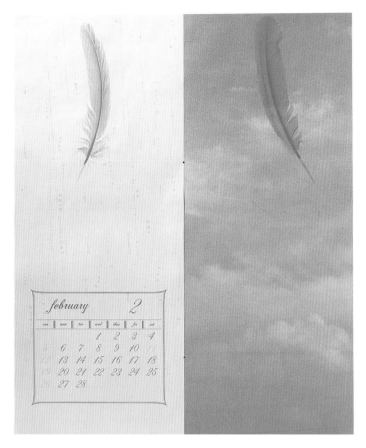

CD, AD, D, I: Issay Kitagawa CL: Graph Co., Ltd. Japan 1995

AD, D: Katsumi Komagata DF: One Stroke Co., Ltd. CL: Tokushu Paper Manufacturing Co., Ltd. Japan 1995

1. CD, AD, D, I: John Sayles DF: Sayles Graphic Design CL: Des Moines Park & Recreation   USA   1996

2. CD: Daisuke Konno AD, D: Hiroaki Konya DF: Kokoku Nojo CL: Sanwa Bank   Japan   1996

1. **D, I**: Akihiko Tsukamoto **CL**: Yamato Inc.   Japan 1996

2. **AD**: Rick Lambert **D**: Mike Barker / Ben Phillips **DF**: Rick Lambert Design Consultants **CL**: Dromaius Australia   Australia 1996

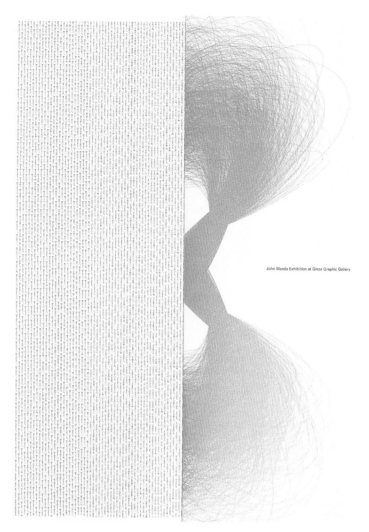

John Maeda Exhibition at Ginza Graphic Gallery

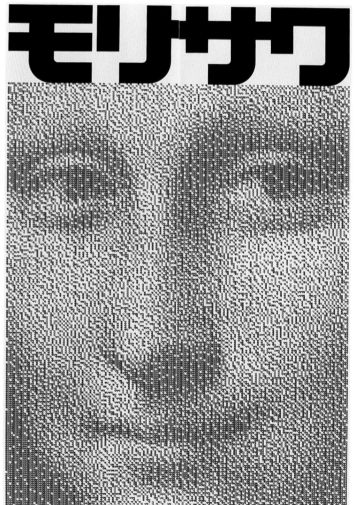

AD, D: John Maeda CL: Ginza Graphic Gallery   USA 1996   M

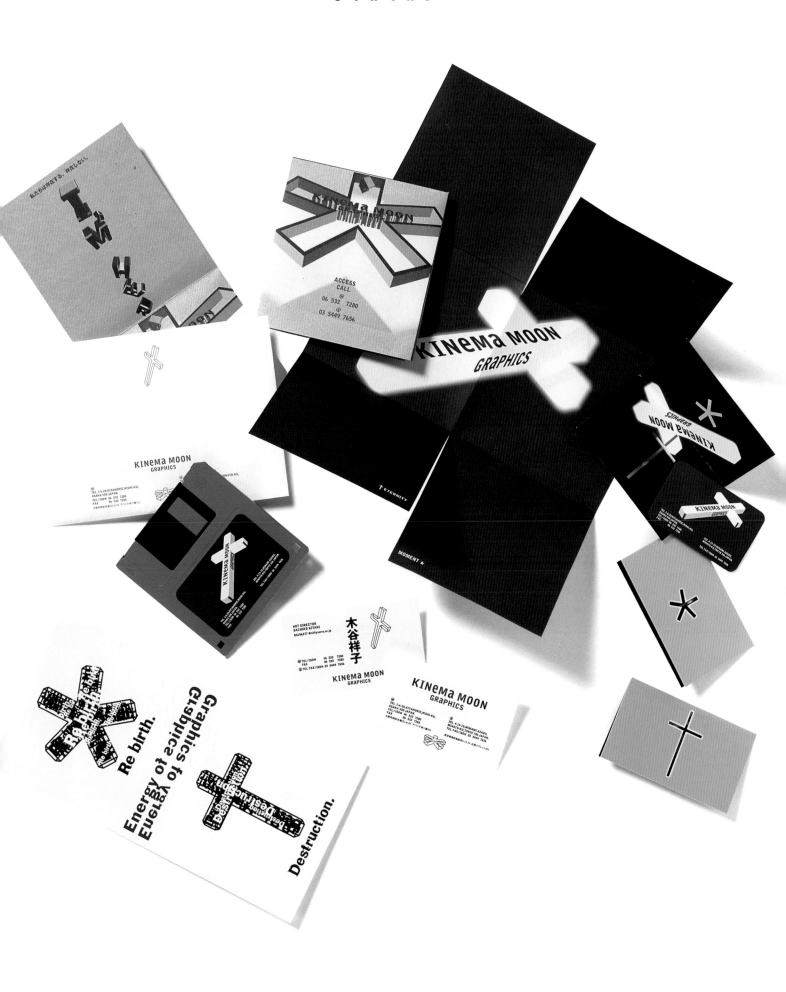

CD, AD, D, I: Vision Network Co., Ltd.   Japan

D, P: Masami Nagai CL: M. A. D. Japan 1996

CD, AD, D: Peat Jariya AD, D: Scott Head DF, CL: Metal Studio Inc.   USA 1994

CD, AD, D: Terry Greene P: John CW: Gay Griffin DF: Design Factory CL: Lime Street Ireland 1996

1. **AD, D**: Barbara Casadei **CL**: Arianova Rock Fantasy   Italy   1996

2. **CD, AD**: Stefan Sagmeister **D**: Veronica Oh **DF**: Sagmeister Inc. **CL**: Aerosmith   USA   1995

1. CD, AD, D, I: John Sayles CW: Wendy Lyons DF: Sayles Graphic Design CL: AIGA Wichita   USA 1996

2. CD, AD, D, I: John Sayles CW: Allison Bishop DF: Sayles Graphic Design CL: Principal Residential Mortgage   USA 1995

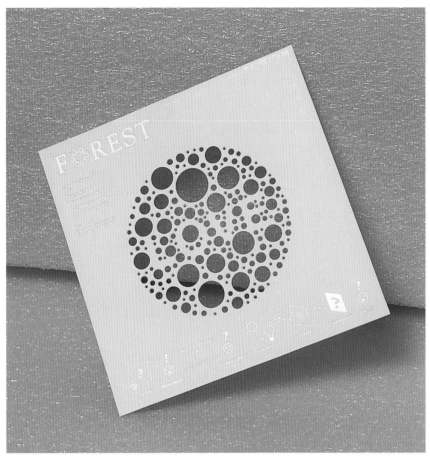

1. CD: Noriyuki Tanaka CD, D, Artist: Makoto Orisaki CL: Science Museum   Japan 1996 *No color
Can you see the message? メッセージが見えますか？（Answer : P220）

2. CD: Noriyuki Tanaka CD, AD, D: Makoto Orisaki I: Yumiko Noguchi CL: Science Museum   Japan 1996
Card is inflated by blowing into it from the back. 後ろから息を吹き込むと立体的になります。

M   1. CD, D: Robert Bergman - Ungar AD: Giles Dunn DF: Bergman - Ungar Associates CL: For Life Records   USA 1996

2. D: Takao Yamashita CL: Beauty and Beast   Japan 1996

CD: 1. Petit Mangin / Pfaffli / Clavelly / 2. Alexandre Petit Mangin DF, CL: La Vache Noire France 1996

1. CD, AD, D, I: John Sayles D: Jennifer Elliott P: Bill Nellans CW: Wendy Lyons DF: Sayles Graphic Design CL: American Heart Association   USA 1996

201

2. AD, D: Katsumi Komagata DF: One Stroke Co., Ltd. CL: F. D. C. Products Inc.   Japan 1996

AD: Nick Crosbie **D:** Simon Clark **CL:** Inflate   UK   1996   F   M   F

1. **AD, D:** Akira Sumi **CL:** Men's Bigi Co., Ltd. Japan

2. **AD, D:** Akira Sumi **CL:** Men's Bigi Co., Ltd. Japan 1996

1. **AD, D:** Juliet Zeif **P:** Theo Fridlizius **CL:** Theo Fridlizius Photography   USA   1996

2. **CD, AD:** Sean Perkins / Simon Browning **D, Typographer:** Mason Wells **DF:** North **CL:** Syn Production Co.   UK   1996

1. Ink supplier: Toyo Ink MFG. Co., Ltd. **CL:** M. A. D.   Japan
*Recycled paper and soya ink　再生紙チップボード／ソイビーンインク(食物性インク)使用

2. CD, AD, D, I: Carlos Segura **DF:** Segura Inc. **CL:** [T-26] USA 1996

co·ex·ist
DESIGNED & PRODUCED BY YAT
SPRING/SUMMER COLLECTION 95

DECEMBER 1994
7:00 PM (DOOR OPEN 5:00PM)
CO-EXIST SHOP
5-47-6 JINGUMAE·SHIBUYA-KU·TOKYO
PHONE:03-5775-5863

BUY MORE SOCKS

共存
co·ex·ist
AUTUMN COLLECTION 94

CD, AD, D, P, I: YAT CL: Coexist Japan
*Yellow vinyl tape

CD, AD, D: Tom Bonauro P: Christine Alicino CL: George USA 1993-1995

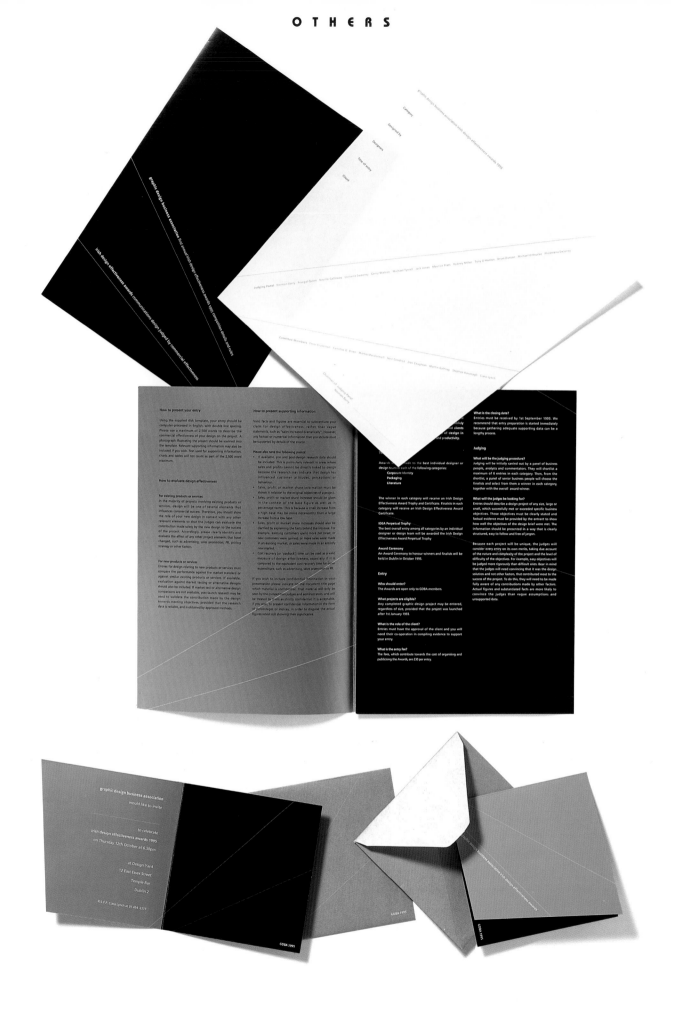

CD: Stephen Kavanagh AD, D: Amanda Brady P: Walter Pfeiffer Studio DF: Design Factory CL: Graphic Design Business Association Ireland 1995

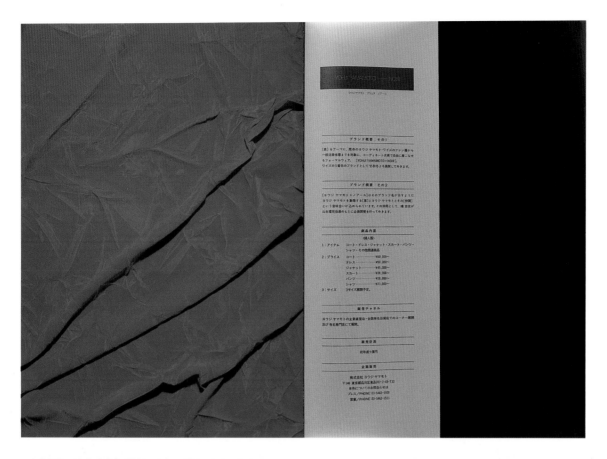

CD, AD: Katsu Asano D: Kinue Yonezawa P: Taka Kobayashi / Kazumi Kurigami DF: Asa 100 Company CL: Yohji Yamamoto Co., Ltd.   Japan 1995

1. **AD**: Antonella Mandoli **D**: Barbara Longiardi / Giovanni Pizzigati / Massimo Arrigoni / Stefania Adani **CL**: Nike Italy   Italy 1996

2. **AD, D**: Barbara Casadei / Massimo Arrigoni **CL**: Nike Italy   Italy 1996

1. CD, AD, D, I: John Sayles CW: Jack Jordison DF: Sayles Graphic Design CL: James River Paper Corporation   USA 1995

2. CD: Emine Tusavul AD: Faruk Baydar DF: T. T Reklam Hizmetleri CL: Limon Co.   Turkey 1995

CD, AD, D, CL: Alto Campo Company   Japan

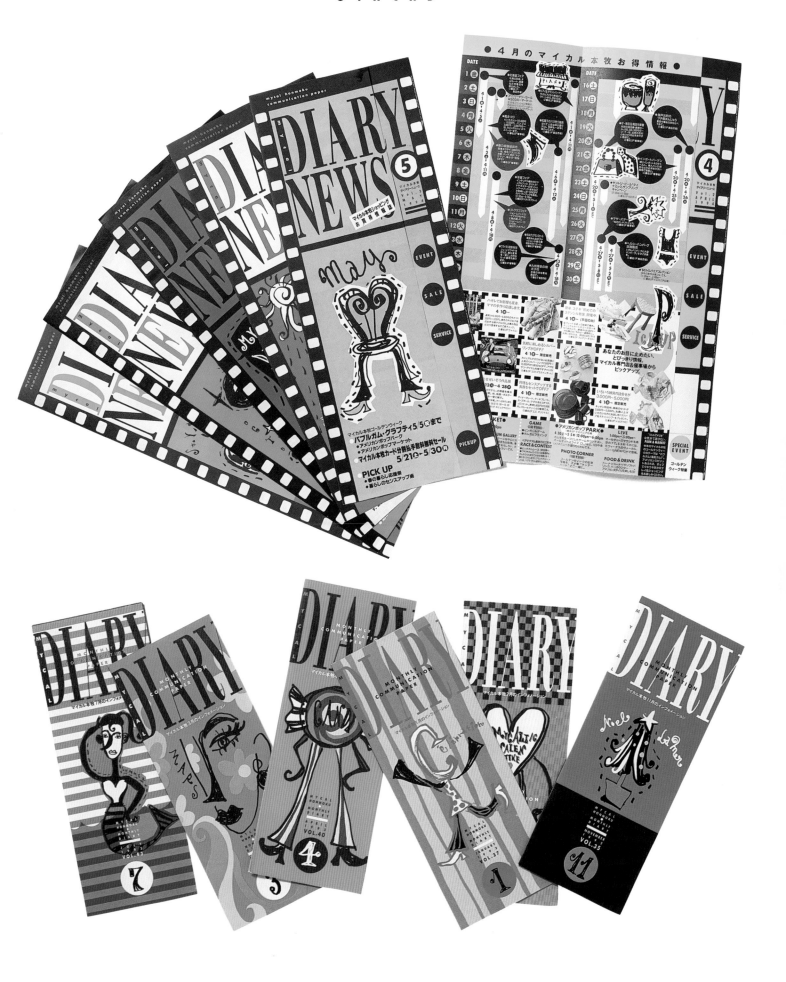

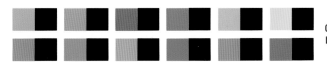

CD, AD: Sayuri Takahata D: Kaoru Matsui / Noriko Kubo
I: T. Sarry CL: Mycal Honmoku Japan 1992-1995

CD, AD, D: Hidenori Okahashi DF: Lotoath Deisgn Studio CL: Pros. Japan 1996

AD, D: Katsunori Hironaka DF: Hironaka Design Office CL: K. Corporation Japan 1993

1. **AD**: Charles Shields **D**: Juan Vega / Laura Thornton **DF**: Shields Design **CL**: Valliwide Bank   USA   1993

2. **AD, D**: Katsunori Hironaka **DF**: Hironaka Design Office **CL**: Murata Clinic   Japan   1993

index of submittors

Jacket Design
Hajime Kabutoya

Art Direction & Design
Douglas Gordon

Editor
Tomoe Nakazawa

Photographer
Kuniharu Fujimoto

Coordinator
Naoko Arai

English Translator
Sue Herbert

Typesetter
Yutaka Hasegawa

Publisher
Shingo Miyoshi

1 & 2 Color Design Collection 1
1 & 2 色デザインコレクション 1

2005年7月11日　初版第1刷発行

発行所　ピエ・ブックス
〒170-0005　東京都豊島区南大塚2-32-4
編集　Tel: 03-5395-4820　Fax: 03-5395-4821
e-mail: editor@piebooks.com
営業　Tel: 03-5395-4811　Fax: 03-5395-4812
e-mail: sales@piebooks.com

印刷・製本　株式会社サンニチ印刷

この本の売上の一部は、出品者の方々のご厚意によりユニセフに寄付されます。
Part of the sales of this book will be donatedto UNICEF by courtesy of the submittors.

ご協力のお願い：今回の書籍出版にあたり調査をしましたが、最終的に連絡をとることができなかった出品者の方がいらっしゃいます。
どなたか連絡先をご存じの方がいらっしゃいましたら、お手数ですが小社編集部までご一報下さい。

Please help... Despite exhaustive investigation in preparing this book, these are still some submittors that we have been unable to contact.
We ask anyone who knows how to contact these people to please notify our editorial staff, and thank you in advance for your assistance.